WEON

AN INSIDE LOOK AT MICHIGAN'S FINAL FOUR RUN

BY **JOSH BARTELSTEIN**

BLOG
into**BOOK**

Published in the United States of America

ISBN: 978-1619849914

To view more photos and videos get the interactive e-book at BlogIntoBook.com/Michigan

TABLE OF CONTENTS

THE 2010-11 SEASON

FINAL FOUR WEEK

THANK YOU

This blog into book would not have been possible without a couple of people. First off, coach Beilein, who always encouraged giving the fans an inside view. He also knew Mrs. Beilein really enjoyed reading them and that was my "in"! You will read about coach B over and over in this book, but the only thing you need to know about him is that he is an even better person than a coach, and you all know how good of a coach he is!

Tom Wyrwot, our Sports Information Director. He was in charge of the blogs and they really were his idea to start with. No better SID in the business and also a great, great guy. TDUB, none of this happens without you.

The fans! This blog into book was created for you. I wanted you to see what goes into playing college basketball at the University of Michigan. There is no place like it and the fame this blog gave me comes from you. My hope is you guys don't just read this book to revisit the Final Four year, but really read it from start to end. Get to know the characters and the journey this program took to reach dominance. There were a ton of laughs, tears, and smiles along the way, but it was a unique path, and our path.

And last, but not least, my teammates. What these four years taught me more than anything else was how special being a part of a team is. Giving and feeling appreciated for something bigger than yourself is something every kid needs to experience. I had fifteen best friends I got to see every day. Over the three years of this blog, we didn't have a ton of turnover—these guys will be my best friends the rest of my life. This book can only say so much, but what we saw, experienced, and lived is a combination between student, athlete, and rock star.

With that, enjoy the book. Inside, you will see every blog I ever wrote; numerous new ones; pieces from Tim, Trey, Zack, and Stu, and behind-the-scenes videos and pictures. My favorite parts are all the videos of us on the plane, at the pep rallies, and the footage from the fans celebrating. You will see every angle there is to see. What the coaches were doing, the fans in Atlanta, and of course, us. If you didn't get to come to ATL, by the end of this you will feel like you did.

PS: I need to give a big thanks to all my high school English teachers at Phillips Exeter Academy and Highland Park. They will be SHOCKED to hear I'm a published author and I wrote it all by myself! So Mrs. Elman, Mrs. Schwartz, Mr. Swanson, and Ms. Case, I hope you have a big smile! All those red marks on my paper paid off.

INSIDE THIS BOOK

I get the question all the time: How did this blog/book start? The funny thing is this blog was started at the same time the Michigan basketball program was redefining itself. It wasn't in Ann Arbor, or even the United States, but the rebirth of Michigan basketball, and the birth of the Bartelstein blog took place in a hotel in Belgium. I was sitting in my room writing about our trip, and the coaches were meeting in a conference room deciding what values they wanted to use to define a Michigan basketball player. At the time, we the players, had no idea Wolverine Excellence was being created and I'm pretty sure the coaches had no idea my blog was being created (for the record they have always enjoyed it). Wolverine Excellence has taken on a little life of its own (WEON), but don't doubt for a second that the reason Michigan Basketball is now an elite program has a lot to do with the culture defined in that conference room in Belgium.

The question many of you may be asking now is: Why were you in Belgium? The summer going into my sophomore year—the 2010-2011 season—we took a summer tour playing four games in Belgium. College teams are allowed to do this every four years, and more than anything else it's a great bonding experience. We played four REALLY good teams and went 1-3. The media back home said it was an embarrassing trip; a waste of time, but to this day that trip may have been the single most important month of Michigan basketball. It allowed our extremely young team to come together, but also the culture I mentioned earlier was created.

Some readers will have stopped reading by now because they see culture and think "corny". Who really needs a culture? Just recruit stars! Our culture is what makes everyone understand what a privilege it is to play at the University of Michigan and under coach Beilein. We start implementing it to the freshmen the day they walk in the door in the summer, but they don't understand how special it is until midway through their freshman year, and that's good. Anything that is as sacred as a team's culture should not be picked up right away. You need to see it in action, on the court, in the classroom, and in the community. If they understood it right away, then something would not be right.

Getting the freshmen to follow this culture is way easier than you would think. If Cazzie Russell, Glen Rice, Juwan Howard, Zack Novak, and Trey Burke all understood what it meant to be a Michigan Man, then how can a freshman who hasn't achieved a thing yet in college not follow in line? The brand of the block M is bigger than you or me or any of those guys listed above—the program and university will always be bigger than any one player.

Our culture is defined from five words: Unity, Passion, Appreciation, Integrity, and Diligence. We refer to it as UPAID. Those words appear on t-shirts, the walls of Crisler, and anywhere our coaches can think of. The point is to see it over and over again because that is who we are. Those words create our Wolverine Excellence motto, which is where the WEON shirts came from.

So the reason this book is special to me is because it directly traces the rebirth of this program. Progress isn't steady—there were ups and downs, but nothing you ever want in life comes without a ton of hard work. If you read this entire blog, not only will you laugh a lot, but you can track how this program went from under .500 to an NCAA tourney team to Big Ten champs to National Finalist. That kind of jump doesn't happen-that's elite!

FOREWORD BY ZACK NOVAK

I will never forget that day. It was February 3rd, 2008, and I was sitting in my high school gym for study hall doing whatever homework I had. My high school coach handed me his cell phone and said, "It's Michigan." At that exact moment I was sold, and I hadn't even spoken one word to Coach Beilein yet. Michigan had one scholarship come open in the middle of the season and they were looking for the right person to fill that spot. Coach and I spoke several times over the next month before he finally offered me the scholarship. Throughout that process, he was insistent on one thing: he had the plan to turn Michigan Basketball around. He had turned around every program he had been at before and he was sure he would do it again. He just needed guys who believed in him and his vision. Time and time again, he spoke about wanting "good guys" who would do things "the right way." There would be no cutting corners and it would be a process. At the time, I honestly had zero idea how I would fit into the equation, but I couldn't help but believe in his plan.

Success wasn't supposed to happen that fast. The core of the 2008-09 team was made up of guys from a team that had won ten games the year before. Our recruiting class wasn't highly regarded at all. In fact, the first time I walked into the locker room, I remember Manny asking me if I was a football player recruited to play fullback. I also vaguely remember someone posting a picture of Ben Cronin, Stu, and I on TheWolverine's message board sarcastically stating that we were the "future of Michigan Basketball." Looking back, we were able to defy the odds that year for a few reasons. First, we had a group of returning players who were hungry to prove that they were better than they had shown the year before, mixed with a group of freshman whom literally everyone looked over. Coach Beilein always wants his players to have a chip on their shoulder, and it wasn't very hard to convince that group to have one. We also had two all-league guys who stepped up that year in Manny Harris and Deshawn Sims. After being thrown for a coaching change early in their careers, they handled it like professionals and played great. Finally, and most importantly, we had two senior leaders in David Merritt and CJ Lee who were consistently solid. They bought into Coach Beilein's vision and kept every single guy on that team on track day in and day out with "no lapses and no discrepancies," as CJ loved to say. With great leadership starting at the top with the coach and trickling down to the captains, two stars, and a hungry group of guys, we were able to end Michigan's NCAA Tournament drought and even win a game in it.

Michigan Basketball was finally poised to make a potential run back to the Final 4. We returned the core of the previous year's team and added a great recruiting class. A preseason Top 15 ranking had the fans and media excited. Behind the scenes, the coaching staff had some real concerns, though. Dave and CJ were solid players on the court, but surely we could make up their production. They did, however, make up 100% of the leadership within the team. They were so good at what they did that no one really had to lead the previous year. I remember having several talks with Coach Beilein leading into that season about taking on more of a leadership role. From my perspective, it was almost surreal to think that I was having conversations about being the captain of Michigan a little over a year after I was scratching and clawing to even get a scholarship offer. Needless to say, I was excited about the new challenge. I had spent the last year silently observing two great leaders, picking up things that I knew I would use to shape my own leadership style someday. I felt like I was ready. Unfortunately, the year did not go as anyone expected. In the previous year, everything that could go our way seemed to do so. During the 2009-10 season, it was the complete opposite. It was one of the most humbling experiences of my life. After a disaster of a year, we lost our two best players and leading scorers. Everyone on the outside thought that Michigan Basketballwas no closer to a restoration than we were two years previously. They may have been right, but we had guys in that locker room who believed in our coach's vision.

The offseason preceding the 2010-2011 campaign can best be described as the "Summer of Shakeups." Coach Beilein brought in two new assistant coaches, Bacari Alexander and Lavall Jordan, and promoted his personal assistant Jeff Meyer to a coaching role. Our roster consisted of two seniors, six sophomores, and six freshmen. Though many people were rightfully bearish on our odds to succeed that year, our youth allowed us to have a certain naivety that we could compete with anyone. The new staff spent the time leading up to the season injecting our young team with confidence and defining to us what it meant to play Michigan Basketball. That culture can simply be defined by five core values: integrity, unity, passion, diligence, and appreciation. The blueprint for a successful program was laid in front of us. Much like CJ and Dave in our freshman year, it was now up to Stu and I to bring that consistent leadership to make sure our young team lived and played with these values in mind each day. We had a decent start to the year, but when conference play began, things were looking bleak. We started off 1-6 in the Big Ten and lost to then-ranked-number-one Kansas in that same time period. Most teams would have crumbled, but Coach Beilein kept everyone believing. After an embarrassing loss at Northwestern, I'll never forget him telling us, "This team will play in the NCAA Tournament." Again, that naivety paid off. Through that entire losing streak, we kept a positive attitude and, more importantly, kept working our tails off in practice. After that kind of start, we were lucky enough to have an away game at the Breslin Center. We hadn't won there since the mid '90s. Fans on both sides were talking about the thousand-day-plus streak since Michigan had beaten MSU in basketball or football. I only had one message for the team: we were going to go into East Lansing, get a win, and the entire season would immediately be turned around. That one game was all we needed.

In hindsight, that win was bigger than a season-saving win. It was a program-shifting game. The rest of the season, we could see Coach Beilein's vision begin to become a reality. We played some of the best basketball in the country, earned another tournament berth, and came about two inches away from sending number one seed Duke to overtime in the round of 32. With such a young team, the future looked very bright. Unfortunately, part of the territory that goes along with building a championship program is that having guys leave for the NBA is a part of life. Darius had earned his opportunity to play at the next level and he took it. With him, we were a preseason top five team in many people's opinions. Without him, some people weren't so sure. The guys inside of our locker room were sure, though. We had a coach we believed in and teammates we had fought alongside with and won. The foundation for the program was solidifying.

Leading into my senior year, two big questions kept coming up. The first concern that was voiced by many was our drop-off in success after my freshman year. The situations were so different. The credibility of our leadership within the locker room was on a higher level. My sophomore year, I was a first-time captain trying to lead guys who were older than I, and Deshawn was also a first-time captain. Leading into our senior year, I had two years of captain experience and Stu had one. There was absolutely no chance either one of us would allow for that type of slip-up. The other problem people potentially foresaw was a little more warranted. We had lost our record-setting point guard from the year before. Who would run the team? That question was answered to me in one of our first open gyms that summer. Freshmen come in every year and typically do one of two things in open gym: shoot it every time they touch it, regardless of the score, or never shoot at all. Trey Burke definitely did not fall into the latter category. In the first game, we came down at game point and Trey stopped behind a ball screen from NBA-plus range and hit a shot. I told him, "Good shot, but at game point we can get better." In the second game, we were in the same situation. Trey drives, spins, throws up a floater, and hits it. I said nothing. We found ourselves at game point again in the third game. Trey came down and hit a near impossible step-back to win it. After that, I told him, "If we get to game point again, shoot that ball in!" As far as I was concerned, we were poised to have a special year. We had experience returning at nearly every position and a strong point guard.

Our goal that year was to win a Big Ten championship. We said it every day after practice. After a loss at Michigan State in early February, we had seven games remaining with an 8-4 record. I remember Coach Jordan calling me into his office and he had our schedule pulled up on a monitor in his office. I typically took things one game at a time, so I didn't even know who we had coming up. He showed me our upcoming games and said, "We can run the table here and we have a real shot to win the league." The hardest game we had left was a home game against OSU, which we won in the craziest game I had ever been a part of in the Crisler Center. We did drop our final home game to Purdue, but were still able to clinch a share of a Big Ten title during a year in which the conference was the strongest in the country.

So much had changed within a short amount of time. Four years before, the program hadn't been to a tournament in over a decade. The university built a brand new training center and renovated a badly outdated Crisler. As Bo said, "Those who stay will be champions." All of the fans who stayed with Michigan Basketball were now rooting for championship teams again. The future of the program had never been brighter, as Coach Beilein's vision was fully coming to fruition. Unfortunately, for the final team Stu and I captained, we did not have the ending we dreamed of. As a kid you envision making a run to the Final Four. As a fan there is no better time of year than watching your team make a deep tournament run. Michigan Basketball had broken the tournament drought with three bids in four years and won a Big Ten Championship. There was one final step needed to solidify itself back as a premier program in the country. We needed to make a run in March.

EXCERPT FROM TREY BURKE

Growing up in Columbus, I wasn't necessarily a Wolverines fan, but when I was offered a scholarship, I jumped at the opportunity. The team made it to the second round of the NCAA tournament the year before I arrived and I was excited because I thought I could take the program even further. As a kid, I had heard about the Fab Five, all the swagger, and the storied Michigan tradition. I wanted to bring the program back to its glory days. I didn't know if the guys thought I could come in and immediately take over for Darius Morris, but I was up for the challenge. I'd been told that I was too short, or not good enough to play at the highest levels my whole life, so I always had a chip on my shoulder. I was determined from the minute I stepped foot in Ann Arbor.

It was unbelievable to win a Big Ten championship as a freshman and I think the team trusted me after that to be the leader and come through in the clutch. I definitely thought about leaving after that first year because it had always been my dream to play in the NBA, but I still had something to prove. A first round loss in the NCAA tournament was not how I wanted my Michigan career to end. Once I made my decision to come back, I felt like nothing could stop us. We went through some rough stretches throughout the Big Ten season, but when the NCAA tournament started and everything was on the line, we were at our best. I wasn't surprised that we made it to the championship game. I felt like we could do that from day one that year. I was proud to say Michigan Basketball was back!

EXCERPT FROM TIM HARDAWAY JR.

Growing up in Miami, Florida, I never knew a single thing about the University of Michigan. I was always an ACC type of guy who loved the Duke, UNC, and FSU etc. type of college. All I ever knew was the U—also known as the University of Miami. FSU and UM were the two big schools in my state that were big rivals; and every game I went to when those two teams played was something I would never forget. But when playing basketball in Miami an opportunity came along to play at the University of Michigan. Once I heard of the school my first reaction was "Michigan? Why would I go there?" I never realized how big and popular the school was because I grew up as a southern kid— until my dad threw a little knowledge to me. When I took my visit to Michigan I didn't know what to expect, I had mixed emotions until I went to the Michigan vs. Duke game in Ann Arbor. Once I saw that game and how the fans were, I kind of knew where I wanted to be; and that was in Ann Arbor.

During the recruiting process coach Beilein was the ultimate coach for me. The reason I say that is because when he called he never talked about basketball; it was always about academics and how I was doing in the class room and whether or not I would sit in front of the class. After him asking me those questions and showing me the importance of having an education, I knew his goal for me was to have a life after basketball. I immediately felt so comfortable that I verbally committed to the Maize and Blue.

While playing basketball in Ann Arbor, MI, I really loved the fact that not only did my family, teammates, and friends help me with my transition, but the fans, professors, and supporting cast at U of M who were behind the scenes made my time at Michigan a complete success. There were many people who helped me out along the way, but one person who stands out is Zach Novak. He was my co-captain, along with Stu Douglass, and having him as my captain made me more mature as a person, and was one of the reasons why I came to the University of Michigan. Having him in the program made me a better person both on and off the court because he showed me how to handle myself and not to take anything for granted.

My time at Michigan was an epic experience, and I will never forget it. My freshman year was my most memorable year in Ann Arbor because everything that happened that year was unexpected of us. For us to go out there and have the doubters and media place us last in the Big Ten really made us have a chip on our shoulders. After proving a lot of people wrong we ended up finishing 4th in the conference and earned our way to a trip to the NCAA tournament. Also, how can I forget about playing in front of 75,000 people in the Georgia Dome? It was a dream come true and something many professional basketball players have never done. And, last but not least, the winning of a Big Ten conference Championship and bringing it back to Ann Arbor after so many years.

EXCERPT FROM STU DOUGLASS

If I'm being honest, when I first chose to play at Michigan it wasn't as much about the university as it was about playing at the highest level. All I ever wanted growing up playing basketball was to one day play on a national stage against the best competition. At the end of my last AAU summer I saw a lot of high profile schools drop interest in me on the last weekend of the summer, and my dream of a national stage wasn't as bright as I had pictured it. When coach Beilein extended me a scholarship offer I couldn't have been more excited to live out my dream, but throughout my time at Michigan it turned into much more than just playing in the national spotlight. It became about restoring the passion and pride that once surrounded the program and leaving Michigan better than I found it. Being able to be a part of rebuilding a basketball program with the history of great players and teams that Michigan has means more to me than anything I could have ever imagined growing up.

I didn't have nearly the individual college career I aspired for, but sometime within my junior year I realized I could accomplish more for the team and the program than for myself. It wasn't easy to accept, but I took pride in it, and honestly, I figured out that would be the best way to be remembered and get my name in the history books somewhere (I really didn't care where). When the team made their run to the championship game this year, I wanted nothing more than to be a part of it. It almost upset me at times because I couldn't experience it, but throughout their tournament run I was receiving tweet after tweet from fans thanking me and telling me I was a huge part of this run even if I wasn't playing. I still won't take that credit, but it really made me realize how important my four years were at Michigan. Michigan fans have been waiting a very long time to see their team succeed like they did this past year, and it's gratifying to see the passion restored.

You have to really try hard to go through college and neither mature nor learn important life lessons. That said, I doubt I would've matured the way I did and learned what I did playing for any other school under any other coaches. I'm what you call "opinionated." My life motto is similar to that of a Charles Barkley book title, "I May Be Wrong but I Doubt It." When I first got to Michigan I bumped heads with coach Beilein a lot. Eventually, I understood I could stand to learn a thing or two from coaches Beilein, Bacari, Lavall, and Jeff if I stopped trying to fight them all the time. Taking responsibility for your own actions is a foreign concept to some people. I realized the quicker I was able to point the finger at myself and say, "You're being an idiot, Stuart, quit making excuses," the smarter I could become and the quicker I could improve as a player. Without the coaching staff, Brian Townsend, and the ups and downs I experienced throughout my four years, it probably would have taken me a little longer to realize the importance of 100% committing to that philosophy—and not just every now and then.

My family went on camping trips a lot when I was growing up. Whenever we were about to pack up and go home, my dad made my sister, brother, and I clean up the entire campsite until it was spotless. He always wanted to leave it clean for the next people to enjoy without having to worry about a mess. He would always tell us, "Leave it better than you found it," and I never understood why he was so adamant about this until we won a Big Ten championship, and I thought back to where it all started my freshman year. Every little bit helps.

THE 2010-11 SEASON

10/15/2010

MEDIA DAY AND THE BEGINNING OF A BLOG

What's up everyone? Hope you all are as excited for the season to start as we are. After we got back from Europe, which was an unbelievable time that we will get into at a later date, sports information director Tom Wywrot asked me about doing a blog this year.

I was a little hesitant at first. Writing a blog is no easy task, plus Mark Titus, who played for that school in Ohio, had a great one. But then I decided it would be a great way to let you guys into my world as a basketball player and as a student.

Everything you see on this blog will be from my perspective as I see it, which could be a good thing or bad thing. If there is anything you want to see on this blog or questions you want answered please send them in to me. My goal is for everyone to understand the life we live and how it is both different and similar to every other student on campus.

You guys will be hearing a lot about Stu (Douglass) and Zack (Novak) in this blog because they are my roommates. We spend a lot of time together from watching our TV shows (we have a lot) to going shopping. Novak looks at clothes online, but does not buy them, while Stu looks at everything online and seems to buy all of it. I think you will see a lot of funny things go on at our house, and I will share as much as I am allowed to share.

Today was media day with the team. You could tell because everyone walked into the locker room with fresh haircuts and a clean shave. Looking clean is essential with Coach B because if you do not look clean then you run the gauntlet. The gauntlet will be referred to a lot. All you need to know is it is a lot of running in a short amount of time.

Matt (Vogrich) and Blake (McLimans) got about one centimeter cut off their hair because they do not want to ruin their look (not sure what exactly their look is). I am pretty sure I got asked the same question in every single way possible during media day. How was Europe? Did you have fun in Europe? Was Europe beneficial for your team? After 40 minutes of answering the same questions over and over, you get a little tired, but we know that it is an important step to starting the season.

After media day, we had an individual with just the guards. Coach Jordan and Coach Meyer put together a really intense 40-minute workout. We got up a lot of shots and did a ton of full speed ball handling. Darius (Morris) can fly with the ball up the court, and when we are doing drills, it is noticeable how fast he is. This was the last workout before the official start of the season. I know everyone is really excited to finish the pre-season work and get onto practice. We officially start Friday (Oct. 15) at 5 p.m.

PRACTICE IS HERE

Hope you all are doing well. We have just finished our first couple days of practice and let's just say they are no walk in the park. Coach B wants to set a tone for the season and so far I'd say he has done a pretty good job because all you have to do is walk in our lockerroom and see everyone sitting in the cold tub. When Tim (Hardaway) is sitting in 50-degree water, you know we are working hard. Tim really does not like cold water and getting him in there is like getting a little kid to get their first haircut: a lot of moaning and screaming.

We have been doing a lot of defensive drill like shell drills, getting through screens and transition defense so that we can set up our offense. We really want to run this year, and the only way you can run is by getting stops.

I thought Coach gave out an amazing stat yesterday. Last year, we averaged 61 points per game in Big Ten games. If we score just three points more a game, we win 10 games in the best conference in the country. They key to scoring more is not in the half court where everyone holds and grabs, but in the open court where Darius (Morris) and Stu (Douglass) are so effective with the ball.

So far one of the most impressive players in practice has been Zack (Novak). It is not because of the hustle everyone loves, or how good of a rebounder he is even though he is 6-3. By the way he is 6-3, not 6-5 and do not let anyone tell you otherwise. Zack worked extremely hard this summer to become a complete basketball player. Last year, Zack was someone who could knock down shots but really could not create off the dribble at all.

I remember telling Zack after the season he needed to spend all summer working on his ball handling. He can shoot it with the best of them and really is a freak athlete – look at last year's dunk contest – but he was not as skilled as he could be. Well, he is as skilled as anyone on our team now. He spent tireless hours in the gym dribbling through cones and shooting pull-up jumpers in the offseason. Zack can create not only for himself in practice, but also for others, which is what we need for him to do. Zack was so committed this summer that he spent a week at the Bartelstein house for "workout week."

Workout week consisted of three workouts a day: speed training, weight training and basketball training. Zack pulled out of the non-basketball drills with a tight back after the first day but still managed to do the basketball drills. Real tough, right? The first day did not go so well for him, but he took pictures of every drill we did. so when get got home he could recreate what we were doing. I would say it worked.

On another note with Zack, he claims he can play multiple sports in college. According to Novak, he can consistently kick 50-yard field goals with ease, which is better than a lot of NFL and college kickers. This all started in Amsterdam when Zack just blurted out he could play both basketball and football at Michigan.

No one on our team believed him, even Tim who will believe anything called him out, but Zack guaranteed it. I suggested we have a contest in between quarters at the Big House but Zack will not agree to that. The only issue with Zack kicking is that he cannot kick extra points or anything close.

Apparently, one of his first extra points in high school he kicked right into the line. The long snapper fell over in pain and missed the rest of the game. So I guess we could use Zack just for the deep field goals because we do not need any more injuries to our linemen

That is it for now. Check back soon and I will update you more on the first week of practice.

J-MO

Five days, seven practices and a lot of running, we have finished our so-called "training camp" as our trainer John DoRosario called it. (I need to devote an entire week of blog entries to John Do at some point).

We have tomorrow off which is much needed for a lot of the team. Guys are banged up and tired from a great first week. I really mean that too, we got so much done since Friday it is amazing. I really feel like our team is so far ahead of where we were last year, partly because of going to Europe but also because our freshmen are picking things up so fast. Evan, Tim, Jon and Colton are all showing why they can get meaningful minutes this year.

One big guy who has really stood out is Jordan Morgan.

J-Mo is a great guy who I've really become close with over the last year. Things have not been easy for Jordan since he arrived on campus but I think he is a lot better off now than anyone could have imagined.

As Jordan will tell you, he will tell you a lot by the way, he gave an arm and a leg to get to this point, literally. He had major surgery on his knee and just when he was getting back from that he injured his shoulder in practice. J-Mo actually plans on writing a book called "I gave an arm and a leg for Michigan Basketball," look for it in stores around 2018. His shoulder injury one of those injuries you don't forget; I was standing near the play and saw his shoulder completely pop out – disgusting. Everyone in the gym will remember that day.

After we all took a summer break, August rolled around and J-Mo was finally back and might I mention better than ever. He was in great shape, had a much-improved jump shot and, most importantly, was just excited to compete again.

By the way, Jordan might have set a record for must one-armed jump shots ever taken. He literally shot one-armed so much I thought he might just switch to it permanently. It was probably better than the jump shot he came in with last June!

The more I thought about it, the more it made sense why J-Mo had invested so much time. When you have something you love taken away for a year you realize how much it means to you. Jordan realized that very quickly. That is why Jordan, along with Darius, was always in the gym shooting before early morning lifts.

Jordan wanted to prove to everyone, and himself, that he was back and he put the work in to have a great season. No one on our team had seen Jordan really healthy. We did not realize what we were missing. Jordan is knocking down jump shots with ease now, running the court like a madman and rebounding like a man possessed.

As a teammate, and more importantly a friend, who saw how hard last year was for him it is really nice to see him healthy and smiling running up and down the court. J-Mo is going to have a really good year and a great career at Michigan On another note I want to give a smut out to Manny Harris who is doing a great job with Cleveland this preseason and has made their opening day roster. We are all proud of you and none of us are surprised how well you have done.

FANTASY FOOTBALL & YOUR QUESTIONS

What's up everyone? Hope you're having a great week. Our first game is less than two weeks away and we cannot wait. As much as we love practice, and I mean love, games are just a little more fun.

I'm sitting here watching Monday Night Football and laughing because everything that could go wrong for Stu's (Douglass) fantasy team has gone wrong. He has Eli Manning (two interceptions), Tony Romo (knocked out) and Roy Williams (done nothing, anyone surprised). He is playing against, Jason Witten (touchdown), Dez Bryant (touchdown) and Hakeem Nicks (two touchdowns). Ha! All day Stu was pumped for this game and it's a disaster. He is sulking eating chips and salsa in his room!

The only person who cares more about football is (Matt) Vogrich. His Sunday depends on how the Bears are doing. Literally as soon as practice ends, he sprints to the computer and gets his stats. Just ask him why Jay Cutler had more completions to DeAngelo Hall than Devin Hester. I would say I feel bad for him, but his roommate Blake (McLimans) roots for the Bills who are not the best themselves. I'll leave it at that since Coach B loves his Bills.

With that ... on to your questions.

> 1. Do you think the team is well-rounded this year? How does it look for the upcoming season in a tough Big Ten?

> This year we are very well-rounded. Last year, we depended on Manny (Harris) and DeShawn (Sims) for so much of our scoring that teams knew going into games if they could shut down those two they would have a good chance to win. This year we have a plethora of scoring options. Stu, Darius (Morris), Zack (Novak), Matt, Tim (Hardaway Jr.), Evan (Smotrycz) and Colton (Christian) are all guys who can put the ball in the basket. Plus, our bigs are getting better and better finishing thanks to the great Bacari Alexander. What makes Coach Beilein's offense so hard to guard is you must account for everyone all the time. Every cut, every play involves all five guys and teams can't lock into any one player. Also, speaking of our guards Darius and Stu, both who are battling for minutes at the point, are shooting lights out in practice. Stu we all know is a big-time shooter who has made big-time shots, but Darius is really shooting the ball well right now also. He is shooting with confidence and from deep with a lot of success.

> As far as the Big Ten goes, it is probably the best conference in college basketball. Four teams in the Top-15 and then anytime you play on the road it is a major test, so there are no easy games. Everyone is going to pick us near the bottom, but I really think we are going to surprise some people. It's too hard to predict wins and losses but I know we are going to give everyone our best shot.

2. Who do you see emerging as leaders on this team? How do you think the leadership will compare to last year's team?

Stu and Zack have done a great job taking leadership of our team. It is hard when you have no seniors on your team, but they have done the best they can to take over as leaders. It is something you learn as you go along, but everyone has a lot of respect for them because of all the time they have put in and the knowledge they have.

3. If/When a team wants to slow the game down to make it a half-court game are we going to be seeing more of the 1-3-1 zone that has become a staple of the defense there at Michigan?

We actually just started putting in the 1-3-1 today. It is something that coach Beilein's teams in the past have had a lot of success with, not just slowing the game down, but getting a lot of steals and fast break points from it. When we play a 1-3-1 we want to make the offense uncomfortable and try and get out and run as much as possible. We will see how it comes along, but I'm sure you will see it often.

4. How much does the team hang together outside of practice? I know you see Stu and Zack all the time, since you room together, but what about the rest of the team?

We are a very close team both on and off the court. Whether guys are at our house, going to a movie or just hanging out there is a good chance we are all together. It is one of those things where teams don't have to be friends, but it makes it a lot more fun when you are close.

5. Since we didn't have Midnight Madness this season, we didn't get to see for ourselves: who is the best dunker on the team this year?

I have to be careful how I answer this question. After Novak won the contest last year, he swore he would never enter a dunk contest again. He was going to go out on top. It is a good thing we didn't have a contest this year because he wouldn't win, he actually wouldn't come in second. Tim and Colton are big-time dunkers. Each of them has moments in practice where you better watch out because they want to come out of nowhere and dunk on you.

6. Do you guys do a lot of backpedaling defensive drills? If so, who's the fastest/best at them?

Interesting question. We do a lot of defensive drills every day, that's one of the biggest changes from last year's practices to this year. I would say Darius is probably the best, with Colton being close behind. I'll have a contest in practice next week and get back to you.

7. How are the "bigs" looking so far? We've got lots of good guards/wings this season, but I always worry about having enough height.

The bigs keep getting better. From where they were in July to where they are now is amazing. They have put in a ton of time with Coach BA and it is really paying off. What people have to realize is that playing-wise they are all freshmen so it takes time. The Big Ten has some great big guys but I know J- Mo, Blake and Jon will battle all day with them because if not BA will let them hear about it.

10/29/2010

WILL FERRELL, THE HEIST AND LOCKED DOORS

It's Friday which means Halloween is right around the corner. I'm guessing Evan (Smotrycz) will have the best costume on our team because he has probably spent the last week planning out exactly what he wanted to wear. If you didn't know, Evan self-proclaimed himself the funniest person on our team on media day, comparing himself to Will Ferrell. Enough said.

Speaking of Halloween, Zack (Novak) and I had a scare the other day.

Before you can understand what happened you must know that we have had a problem with leaving our front door unlocked, (for this reason I can't divulge our address) which we have been working on. Stu (Douglass) is the biggest culprit of this but I'll give him credit he is improving, however I did take away the garage opener from him.

Anyway, Zack, Stu and I constantly joke around that one day our stuff is going to be stolen because anyone can get into our house. It really isn't funny at all. One night Matt (Vogrich), Blake (McLimans), Zack, Colton (Christian) and I went out to dinner at the Black Pearl (great restaurant by the way, highly recommend the salmon). Zack and I were driving Colton back to West Quad and Matt and Blake were going to come hang out.

We pull up to our house and our door is wide open with no one inside. We immediately assume the worst because we knew this day was coming. I go check my room praying they didn't take anything of mine and that the wind just blew the door open. After looking around for 10 seconds, panic sets in that my computer is gone. I yell down to Novak, "my computer is missing" and I assume he is running upstairs to come help me out, but no, he darts right to his room to check out his computer and it's gone.

It just so happened Novak got a brand new MacBook computer earlier that week that he likes more than life right now and if anyone touches it, drops it or scratches there will be a severe penalty. Vogrich threw it onto his bed once and that wasn't a good move. If someone were to steal Novak's computer, it would be very, very bad let's just leave it at that.

Novak and I are flustered. We don't really know what to do, our stuff is stolen and we now realize the robbers also took our video games. It's one thing to take my computer, but to also take my Madden was just crossing the line. Zack was on edge and was close to punching a hole in the wall. At that time Matt and Blake walk in smiling like they are walking in the park. They sense something is really wrong and begin to prod to see what exactly is going on.

At that point Matt and Blake admitted to me they had beaten us to our house and hid all our stuff in their car parked down the street, but Zack was so mad they didn't want to tell him because they weren't sure what he would do to them. Zack is still storming around and they yell to Novak they have his computer and then sprint out of the house so nothing will happen to them.

Five minutes later, they bring the stolen goods back in, Novak is more relieved than mad and just gives his computer a hug. Since this day our house has been on extreme lockdown, we triple-check to make sure every door is locked and sealed shut!

On a more important note, our first game is a week away and I can't wait. We are ready to play against people not wearing a Michigan practice jersey and see how we compare to other teams. I'll get back at you guys soon.

PAUL BUNYAN AND TREADMILLS

We at Michigan are lucky enough to have one of the best training staffs in the country. That staff is primarily made up of Jon Sanderson, our head strength and conditioning coach, and John DoRosario, our athletic trainer. Both of them do a great job getting us ready for the season and also keeping us healthy. Besides that, and the fact they share the same first name, they are quite different people.

Sanderson is a mythological figure. Some say he is related to Paul Bunyan, while others say he can pick up a car with one hand. Point being – he is extremely strong. I have walked into our weight room and seen him benching so much weight the bar was starting to bend and squatting so much I can't even add it all up without a calculator.

On a quick side note, during the preseason we had a different strength and conditioning program this year and it was great for all of us. We got faster, stronger and in better shape than ever before, and most importantly everyone was healthy. I think you will see a lot of guys look different this year on the court from their work with Coach Sanderson.

Okay we are back ...

John DoRosario works out very hard himself. However 'John Do' as we call him doesn't believe in lifting weights – so all of his workouts are body weight movements. He is a big believer in the hip popup and the band walks, just ask Corey Person. We will get back to this in a little while.

Some other things everyone should know about John Do. He holds the record for the fastest ankle-taping job in division one basketball at 12.3 seconds per ankle. He can tape ankles with his eyes closed and one handed. His middle name is Fernando and when we went to Europe this summer we had to call him Fernando because he wanted to blend in better.

Now, let me take you back to last year, the date was February 2nd. We were in Minnesota getting ready to take on the Gophers in a big road game that we would end up winning. I remember this game because Manny (Harris) had a ridiculous dunk in warm-ups that the ESPN camera guy missed and wanted him to do again but we had to leave the court, he was very distraught.

Anyway, before the game some of us wanted to get a workout in at the team hotel, which in Minnesota was really nice. Actually it was the best hotel we stayed in – great breakfast, long beds, and good internet make for a great hotel.

I got up to the workout room with Jordan (Morgan,) Blake (McLimans), Patrick (Beilein), Coach Sanderson and John Do and we all went our separate ways. Pat and I decide to start running on the treadmill, Blake and Jordan hit the weights and John Do let everyone know he is about to start his ultimate workout.

I wish I could tell you what that meant, but I really don't know what the ultimate workout is besides John Do running around doing different lifts with no weight. He then decides part of the ultimate workout must include running on the treadmill with me and Pat so he sets the treadmill at 12.0 mph and starts running.

John Do is making fun of Pat and me for not going fast enough but we just keep running laughing at John Do run. He leaves the treadmill to go do some more hip pop-ups and talk trash about how strong he is getting before returning to run. Now remember the treadmill was still running at 12.0 mph and John Do thought he could just hop right back on like no big deal. Well everyone out there knows you can't just start running at 12.0 mph again, but John Do apparently didn't think this through.

He walked on, still talking about how strong he was getting, when instantly he almost fell flat on his face just catching himself in time. It was by far the funniest moment of the year, Jordan was laughing so hard I thought he might break a rib. Pat had to stop running and I was crying I was laughing so hard. (Another side note – I would be selling Pat short if I didn't include he was a 1,000 point scorer at West Virginia. He always made sure I knew he got a 1,000 points and I know when he sees this it will make his day).

Now I can assure everyone John Do didn't get hurt and played it off like nothing happened, but everyone in there knew how close he came to biting it.

In all seriousness, John Do is a huge part of our team. Everyone realizes how important he is and how hard he works for us all year round. No matter the time of year or day, he is there for us when we need him.

That's all for now, my next blog we will be able to talk about a game for once, which will be nice!

THE MAILBAG

What's up everyone? Since my last post, we played a good game against a very well-coached Saginaw Valley State team. I was very impressed with their defense and how well they got back in transition. Also, their point guard was extremely quick, maybe the quickest player I have seen since I've been here.

Darius (Morris) did a great job of getting him in foul trouble and out of the game – 17 free throw attempts for D-Mo is pretty impressive. With that I hope everyone comes out Saturday night for our first official game as the more fans we have there the better.

Now on to your questions ...

From Drew Question: How much do you guys work on defensive positioning, body positioning, and footwork in practice?

Answer: We do a ton of defense in practice every day. Different shell drills where we jump to the ball and make sure we are in the gaps. Our goal is to not let anyone get into the paint. This has been a huge emphasis for us this year as we try and be a great defensive team.

Question: What do the players think about exhibition games? Are they good for "getting the bugs out" and trying different lineups, or are they just a waste of time?

Answer: For me there really is no difference. Once you get to exhibition games, they are the real deal. We have fans watching us, refs on the court and finally get to put on our new uniforms, which I think are really cool. I've seen people saying they don't look very good but they are much lighter than last year and the new trim is a lot better.

Question: How much coaching happens on the bench during a game?

Answer: There is a lot of coaching that goes on during the game, but it is different kinds of coaching. Once you get to the game, you just want your players to play freely and compete. The worst thing for us to do is think about everything you are doing. Coaches are always reminding us about scouting reports on the bench and other key points that are in our game plan. Still, there is more coaching in practice than a game.

From Champswest Question: Who do you predict will lead the team in three-pointers made?

Answer: Tough question. We have so many great shooters. Stu, Zack, Matt, Tim and Evan are the five guys who will compete for the most makes. I'm going to take Stu in a close one as he has been on fire in practice.

From Chad Question: My question is about Matt Vogrich. Last year he was behind Manny Harris on the depth chart, didn't get much PT, and struggled a bit on the defensive end keeping up with more athletic players. How much has he improved over the off-season and what can we expect from him this year? What have you been seeing from him in practice? Is he a potential starter on this year's team?

Answer: In an article I was interviewed for ESPN, I picked Matt as the player that was going to surprise the most people this year. He was stuck behind a great player last year and didn't ever get a rhythm to really be judged. I know Matt worked his tail off this summer because I was with him in the gym every day. You guys saw his pull-up jump shot in the exhibition game and how effective that worked. When you have such a lethal shot as Matt does, it makes the rest of your offensive game that much easier. The key for Matt is not to be defined just by his offense. Matt has gotten a lot better as a defender and he can really rebound around the basket. People think he is small and doesn't mix it up inside, but he led our team in rebounding in Europe and I expect him to get lots of key boards during the year as well.

From Cobey Question: I'm a sophomore at Highland Park High School. Turns out at I have the same pre-calculus book that you did. Looks like I got a $38 autograph and a pre-calc book at book sale this year. Good Luck this year, and I know that Coach Harris is proud to have coached a Michigan basketball player.

Answer: Cobey the only advice I can give you is don't use any of the answers in that book, because there is a real good chance they aren't right if it is truly my book. Let's just say math has never been my favorite or best subject.

I'll be back later this week with some good stories about our team. It's been great hearing how much people have enjoyed the blog so far. The feedback has been great and that's all I am aiming for.

Hopefully I'll see you all Saturday night.

THE JOYS OF OWNING AN AUTOMOBILE

It's that time of the year again.

Yes, college basketball is about to kick into full swing, the NFL now plays games on Thursday nights (didn't know this in time for my fantasy matchup) and yes the holiday season is right around the corner. You walk into any store now and the holiday sales are up, the red and green ornaments. It just makes you smile.

For some people on our team, their presents came early. I'm specifically talking about Jordan Morgan. By the way, was I right or was I right with my prediction of J-Mo coming through big. I know it was one game and it was an exhibition but still 15 rebounds is a huge amount against anyone.

Anyway, J-Mo got a brand new car about a month ago as his Christmas came early. I literally can't tell you how excited he was. Since the day the season ended last year all I would hear about was the countdown for his new car to arrive. Two people may have been almost as excited as J-Mo. Darius (Morris) because they are roommates and that means he has a ride everywhere and Zack (Novak) because now he never has to pick up the freshmen ever again.

I was a little skeptical with Jordan getting a new car. For one, (Matt) Vogrich lent his car to Jordan for a day last summer and it came back with no gas pedal. I kid you not, Jordan literally stepped on the gas so hard, if completely fell off. For this reason, no one ever would let Jordan borrow their car to drive. He was banned.

Before we can continue with Jordan's car, I must first tell you a quick story about Manny's (Harris) car. One day last year after practice, for some reason Manny let Matt and I take his care back to the dorms. There was no reason why we needed it and no reason for him to give it to us, but we decided to take it.

This was the dumbest choice ever, we had nowhere to park it and we didn't need it, I clearly remember telling Matt this was going to be a disaster. Sure enough, I was right because we couldn't get the car to go into reverse and the brakes didn't work real well. I was pretty sure we weren't going to make it back to the dorm.

After about an hour of driving in a circle we finally park the car. To make a long story short, when we went back to get the car in the morning it was gone. Literally, nowhere in sight, peaced out, adios. We had somehow managed in a span of 12 hours to mess up the brakes and gotten Manny's car towed. Good work for two freshmen, you think we were a little scared to go to practice the next day?

Now back to J-Mo's car. So not to long ago Jordan showed up in a beautiful Trailblazer. It was shiny, clean and ready for Jordan to wreck havoc in. He gave me a ride a couple days after he got it and I was trying to roll down the window. Next thing I know, Jordan is screaming don't touch the window you are going to ruin my tints. He was so mad; it was like his tints were the most important thing ever. It would be like breaking your parents TV or something. At the time, I had zero idea what he was talking about. I'm a kid from the suburbs of Chicago, we don't have tints. Anyway, I can assure everyone his tints aren't ruined and I know no more than I ever wanted to know about tinted windows.

Another problem arose over this weekend for the new Trailblazer. As you all know, football Saturday in Ann Arbor can get a little crazy and finding a place to park is no easy task. Well, J-Mo decides it is best to park at our house and then just walk to Crisler for practice. (Please note, west quad where Jordan lives is closer to Crisler than our house but he still wanted to park at our pad, I can't explain this part to you) Anyway, there are no spots left at our complex and he decides to park illegally on the street since no one was going to check on a day like today.

Funny thing happened on our walk back from practice. That beautiful, shiny Trailblazer was MIA. At first no one realized this, but as we approached the house, I ask Jordan where exactly did you park? He proceeded to say some words I wont' share and launch his water and Gatorade bottle at our garage door.

I couldn't stop laughing and just walked inside. Next thing I know I hear Zack screaming for Jordan, isn't that you car as a tow truck is just driving down the street. It was like out of a movie, Jordan starts running after the tow truck trying to get him to stop. Sure enough, Jordan got him to drop the car for a much smaller fee.

It is now getting late which means I need to go to sleep. It is Free Throw Friday with the Michigan basketball team. This means we will all make 100 free throws before most people start their day of work.

Lastly, I promised my three younger sisters I would give them a shout out and my mom was getting made at me because this is blog 8 and there has been zero mention.

So Morgan, Courtney and Kirby I'm very excited to see you all this weekend as they are coming to watch us play USC-Upstate.

So long for now... see you at Crisler!

PHASE II, RSVPING AND THE A.D. DINNER

I hope everyone is doing well. It is crazy that we are done with a month of practice already. At times it has felt long, but overall, it really does fly by quicker than you would think. Despite that feeling, we have officially entered what I call Phase II – no one else but me calls it this but I like it – of the season which means our schedule becomes a little more set in stone.

For the next 16 weeks, we play at least two games a week. This means two days to prepare for a team then a game followed by two more days and then another game. That last day must be a day off NCAA-mandated. So while the first month of practice is all about working on Michigan stuff, Phase II is more about preparing for teams we are about to play.

So, are you ready for Phase II?

On Tuesday this week, we had a very special dinner with our new athletic director, Dave Brandon. Before I get into this dinner, I want to tell a little story about Jon Horford almost not attending. You see about a week before the dinner we got an email asking us to attend and to RSVP back. Well everyone knew right away this was a very important dinner and everyone should reply back right away. When I say everyone, this would include Jon as well.

Turns out, Horford thought we would have training table or practice during the dinner so replied saying he couldn't come. His reply back according to multiple sources sounded something like this. "I'm sorry, but I won't be able to attend dinner on Tuesday. I'll either have practice, training table or a home-cooked meal. Thanks a lot for the invite." That is the Jon Horford we all love. Regardless, we got a chuckle out of it. And don't worry, Jon made it.

The dinner we had was great. Mr. Brandon is an amazing person. There are some people who when they speak they just captivate you. He is definitely one of those people. We found out he was really similar to us and that he was a student-athlete at Michigan who played football and also basketball for a year.

We also learned earlier that day he started a Twitter account and within three hours had over 900 followers. (Zack) Novak was shocked and dismayed that he tripled his following in a matter of hours. It was very cool for us to get to know our athletic director. So many times we hear about all he is doing but we don't really get to know him on a personal level.

I can tell you if you have a chance to meet him I strongly recommend it.

The major point he got across with us is that he is going to do everything in his power to make Michigan Basketball the best program in the country. We couldn't have more support from him and he is showing that with our new practice facility and the soon to be renovated Crisler Arena. In return, we must make him proud and represent the University of Michigan to the highest standard. Something we know and will keep doing.

That is it for now. We have a couple of games this week. Hope to see you all there!

TWO WINS, A BAR MITZVAH AND CLASSIC VOGRICH

Hey everyone.

Since I last blogged, we have won two games against Bowling Green and Gardner-Webb. We played very well in both games with the key being our defense. It is amazing how good our defense looks right now after we struggled so much with it last year.

You have to give our entire coaching staff a lot of credit for this huge improvement. We have spent a lot more time working on defensive concepts and what exactly we are trying to do every possession. You can always hear Coach BA (Bacari Alexander) yelling keep the ball out of the club. (The club is the paint and we are the bouncers, very original)

The roommate combination of Jordan Morgan and Darius Morris has been on fire of late. We need to think of a nickname for this duel! Seriously though, D-Mo is dropping assists left and right and J-Mo continues to show how good he can be. Both of them are showing when you put in a lot of hard work, it pays off.

Another key part of our team so far has been the role of our sixth man – Stu (Douglass). He has really settled into that roll of just coming in and doing whatever needs to be done. Stu can score points in bunches like he did against Gardner-Webb or, as he did against Bowling Green, just show his veteran savvy and settle everyone down.

Transitioning... so on Saturday before the Gardner-Webb game, we stayed at a hotel, something we don't do very often at home unless our game starts early. However this Saturday was different with everyone in town for the football game coach thought it was best to keep everyone together on Saturday night.

We were all in for a surprise when a Bar Mitzvah was taking place in the room next to our film room. Those seventh graders were rocking out and I got to explain to our entire team just what a Bar Mitzvah is. A Kippah and a Tallis aren't exactly things most of our team has seen before, but they are much more knowledgeable now on the Jewish religion.

Some guys on our team wanted to join the party, but I strongly advised against it since we weren't dressed for the part and kind of stick out because of our height. The kids did however manage find to Jordan sitting in the hot tub and apparently had a lot of questions for him.

Speaking of parties – I want to congratulate my cousin Ben on his very own Bar Mitzvah, I'm sorry I cant be there but I'm very proud of you.

Before I can move on to our schedule for next week, we must first talk about what Matt (Vogrich) managed to pull of before the game on Thursday. Matt has a ritual that he always makes his last shot before he leaves the court. So when we were running into the locker room just before the game started on Thursday Matt decided to launch a shot from half court to see if he could knock it in.

The one issue was Juan, who manages Crisler Arena, was starting to clean the backboards with a mop contraption he designed. He always does this before games to make sure there are no smidges on the backboard.

Well, of course Matt managed to hit the mop and it exploded in half. Juan was in shock as one minute he was cleaning the backboard and the next he only had the handle of it in his hand. It was a classic Vogrich moment. I can assure you on Sunday Juan waited until everyone left the court before he began his mopping routine.

Moving forward ... we are off to the Legends Classic where we play Syracuse on Friday. We will start preparing for them on Wednesday, meaning the scout team will start putting in their plays and working on their different defenses.

On Thursday, Thanksgiving for all of you, we will board our charter and head over to Atlantic City. Then we play two games there and will get home some time very late Sunday morning. We will then leave Monday for Clemson where we take on the Tigers in the Big Ten/ACC challenge.

So as you see we are heading right into the thick of our season with a lot of travel. I think you guys will enjoy my blogs on the road because it will offer a lot of insight in to how we travel, which everyone always asks about.

Lastly, It is great to have C.J. Lee back on board as the director of administrative issues, or administrative specialist or, well... you get the idea. He is a great guy who will help the program in a big way.

11/25/2010

WATCHING BIRD, WEAR NO. 2 AND BEING THANKFUL

Hello everyone, you will not believe this, but I'm writing to you from my seat on our charter flight – USA Jet Airlines – as we are just about to take off for Atlantic City and the Legends Classic. I have been told Atlantic City is a much smaller version of Las Vegas. We will see, it has a lot to live up too if that is the case.

What makes this great is I get to document everything I see, especially as I watch Blake McLimans have a complete paranoia attack, as he is really scared of flying. He grabs on to whatever or whoever is around him and holds on for dear life -take off, landing, bumps, really anything. What I've tried to explain to Bird – ironic his nickname is Bird and he hates flying – is if we are going down, we are going down. There is nothing to worry about; it is completely out of his hands. It doesn't comfort him.

Today also happens to be Thanksgiving so I want to wish everyone a very happy Turkey day.

We celebrated Thanksgiving as a team before we left for the airport. Since our families are all over the country, we had an amazing meal at the Sheraton Hotel as a team. For this meal we had a very strict dress code called a No. 2. This means khakis, a button down shirt and nice shoes. For those who were wondering: No. 1 means you must wear a tie, No. 3 means you can wear jeans and finally No. 4 means Michigan sweats. Sounds simple enough right?

Well our team had not been fully equipped to carry out a Nos. 1 and 3, so we went No. 2. We have had issues in the past making sure everyone had black shoes and black socks. We had guys wearing adidas with white socks to nice functions. I can proudly let everyone know that we managed to completely fulfill the requirements of a No. 2 today and everyone looked great ...

Whoa, we just hit a rough patch of turbulence and Bird is holding on so tight to the arm rest his hands are being to turn white ...

Okay, I am back ... during the meal, we all went around the table and said what we were thankful for. There was many shared thoughts, but we realize truly realize how lucky we all are to play for such a great University and coaching staff.

Another reason to be so thankful is the team gear we receive. Since we are one of adidas biggest school's we get some top-notch gear. So far this year we have received several sweat suits, too many shoes to count, hats, shirts and pretty much anything you could possibly want. We are so, so fortunate.

Unlike most teams, we have a ritual when we receive our gear. Bob Bland, hands the gear out and we all sit in a circle and show our true appreciation for receiving the new clothes. It goes with today's blog theme of being thankful.

By far the highlight of receiving the new gear is seeing Tim Hardaway Jr's face when he gets his bag full of gear. It is like a little boy getting his first Christmas present His face just lights up and he really couldn't be happier. Another classic moment I will always remember.

As a team, we are all very excited for our game against Syracuse. It will be a great test, but we are ready. A lot of people say we are too young to compete with the big boys from the Big East, but we are going to Atlantic City for one reason, to win a championship.

Wish us luck and again .. Happy Thanksgiving!

FIRE TRUCKS, THE THIRD FLOOR AND BREAKDOWN

What's up everyone?

What a great win that was last night. Clemson is a very good team and anytime you play on the road it is very difficult. Littlejohn Coliseum was very loud, the Clemson fans make a lot of noise but we stuck together and showed the potential we have to be a very good team.

After struggling against UTEP's defensive pressure, we had a feeling Clemson would try to do the same, but after cleaning some things up for a couple days in practice, you could see the big difference.

Moving to the fun stuff, some interesting things took place in South Carolina. For one, it was a very bumpy ride. Bird (Blake McLimans) was really struggling and when we finally landed he got an ovation from Zack (Novak), Stu (Douglass), Matt (Vogrich) and myself. What freaked Bird out even more was the fact a fire truck was waiting for us when we landed.

Now I tried to tell him this was a good thing because if we did crash they would already be waiting for us, but he didn't fall for that and was freaked out of the thought of being saved by a fireman. But this was not the most interesting/weird thing that happened in Clemson.

Clemson's gym has some unique characteristics to it. I'm not talking about how loud it is, or the fact their colors are purple and orange (interesting note we have played three straight teams with the color orange, has to be a record right?) but the fact we had to take an elevator to our locker room – there was no chance anyone was going to walk up all the stairs.

I have never heard of this or seen this in my life: our locker room was on the third floor of the gym. The only good thing about it was after the game we had a nice celebration riding the elevator back to our dressing room.

I always get questions about what a game day is like on the road. People always say you have so much free time on the road, but that really is far from the truth. So below I'm going to break down a game day for everyone. On a side note, everyone should keep track of the amount of food we eat because it is absurd. This is the work of the great John DoRosario of course.

Game Day at Clemson

(9:00 a.m.) Wake Up.

(9:30 a.m.) Team Breakfast. We usually have an omelet station plus other normal breakfast foods.

10:00 a.m.) Film Session. This film session usually has us watching practice from the day before and also some clips on Clemson. It could be player personnel or it could be certain plays they like to run. Our coaches have every corner covered. We go into every game extremely prepared.

(10:50 a.m.) Break. Time to take a walk outside or just watch some TV. For me this means watch Modern Family, the best show on TV that Stu Douglass turned me onto. I've literally watched 20 episodes in the last week thanks to all the travel.

(12:30 p.m.) Team Lunch. Sandwiches, soup and chips are typical for a game day lunch. We also have a smoothie bar where there is intense competition to make the best smoothie. Last year, I think I took home the award, but this year both Jordan (Morgan) and Jon (Horford) can make a mean smoothie.

(1:30 p.m.) Depart for Arena. We go to the gym to get acquainted with the shooting background and get any last minute preparations done. This means running through plays, getting their out-of-bounds plays down and anything we can think of to get an advantage.

(3:00 p.m.) Relax. Some time to relax or in my case take a quiz. For those of us who are missing a test or quiz, they let us take it on the road as long as an academic advisor is looking over me while I'm taking it. Thanks Professor Malone for letting me take it!

(5:00 p.m.) Pregame Meal. The third meal of the day some people eat, not including snacks, usually has us eating chicken and pasta with some vegetables and potatoes on the side. Always a very good meal. This is also the last time we watch film and go over our game plan one last time.

(7:30 p.m.) Depart for Arena and load up the bus. We are now ready to go to our game and take on Clemson. The bus is silent because everyone is listening to their iPods with Dr. Dre's beats on.

(9:00 p.m.) Tip off at Clemson

(11:30 p.m.) We are celebrating a great win and singing The Victors song in the locker room. After everyone showers, we say hello to some fans and get on the bus to head to the airport. The last meal of the night is served on the bus and it is the biggest of all them. For example, last night in my bag, I had chicken wings, a salad, salmon with vegetables, ice cream and some sort of cake. No one can possibly eat this much.

(3:30 a.m.) After landing at Willow Run airport, everyone is exhausted, but couldn't be happier after a successful night's work. We are on the bus headed back to Crisler to load into our cars and then head right to sleep because in about five hours, class starts.

So there you have it. The Clemson trip in a nutshell.

THE BIG WIN AND THE BIG LOSS

Hope everyone is doing well.

We just came off a really big win on Saturday against a very good Harvard team. Coach Amaker has a team that mirrors the likes of Cornell of last year. We all know what they did last year. Harvard shoots the ball really well, plays an impressive team defense and really has great team chemistry. So, it turned out to be a big win for us.

The two players of the game probably have to be Stu (Douglass) and Zack (Novak). Ah, the roomies. Stu took the game over for a while in the second half and we really needed that. Our offense was really stagnant and Stu picked us up in a big way. Novak had his first career double-double with 12 points and 11 rebounds. Who said he can't play the four man?

I have to make it three, as I need to include Darius (Morris) in the Player of the Game category because he is playing at such a high level. Darius seems to be in complete control of the game and it is amazing to see how big of a jump there is in his game from last year to this year. As coach (LaVall) Jordan always says to us guards, just make winning plays. Darius and Stu are making winning plays.

Switching gears… I almost had one of the best days of my life yesterday. I was taking a great post game nap when Evan (Smotrycz) and Zack came busting into my room with a Hanukkah gift for me. It was one of those scratch and win lottery cards and I really wasn't too excited about it. I was half asleep and scratched off the numbers. At first, because my eyes weren't really open, I told Zack I didn't win, but upon further review I had actually won $5,000. Yes! I legitimately won the lottery ticket game and the house was going nuts.

Evan was running up and down the stairs, I almost fell down all the stairs and Novak was just bitter it wasn't him who won. Next thing I know, Novak gives me another lottery card and I won $10,000. I was calling my friends, even called (Matt) Vogrich to tell him the big news.

In the matter of seconds, I had just become $15,000 richer. I was putting my shoes on and heading off to the gas station when Zack gave me one last ticket to open for HIM. Guess who won again – another $5,000!

Now at this point, I knew something had to be up.

But Evan was acting like I had really just won, calling people he knew and even making arrangements for me to spend the money that night. If basketball doesn't work out for Evan, he should go into acting.

I then noticed Zack had his camera phone out and I became really, really depressed. I went from being the big winner to just winning absolutely nothing. It was all one big prank. Zack and Evan had just gone to the dollar store and bought fake scratch off lottery tickets.

The best part of the story is that a little later, I went to the gas station with Zack and Evan after just to test my luck and I can tell everyone I did actually WIN: one single dollar. So I still came out on top, I guess.

TEAM EFFORT, JON'S HOODIES, LOVE KARMA

Hey everyone, hope you are all staying warm even though I think that's impossible.

We had a huge win over Utah on Friday night that was a total team effort – Darius (Morris) recording another double-double, Zack's (Novak) almost getting another, Tim's (Hardaway Jr) 17 points, to Jon (Horford) playing a great game off the bench.

Another bench contributor – Matt (Vogrich) – had another solid effort, and you can tell his confidence is really on the rise. We all expect all of his jumpers to go in whenever they leave his hand, and he knocked down a few good ones.

All of this is good, but the highlight of the night has to be my man Tim, who just exploded to start the second half and had a monster dunk. I can tell you after the game Tim and I went out to dinner and all he wanted to do was see the replay of his dunk. He couldn't stop smiling.

As I mentioned, a huge key to the game last week was big Jon, who is a unique human being, and we love having him on our team. Jon is guaranteed to make you laugh every practice just because he is well, just Jon. He says some things that make you scratch your head and his fashion sense is one of a kind – he loves the tight jeans and the bright colored hoodies – it's almost a guarantee he wears it to practice.

One thing that is clear however, is how much better Jon has gotten since he arrived on campus. This is partially from working with the great Bacari Alexander, but a lot has to due with the fact of how hard he works. (SIDE NOTE: please follow Coach Alexander on twitter if you aren't already @Bacari34. Trust me, it is worth it)

There is no better example of this then after the Concordia game when Jon went to get up shots, run and shoot free throws while they were cleaning the court. So while the Crisler staff was picking up garbage and media were writing its stories, Horford was getting his hook shot cleaned up. Any time a player as talented as Horford cares as much as he does; it is a scary combination for success. I think Jon is going to be a special player; one all you Wolverine fans are going to be happy to have wearing the Maize and Blue.

And now ... back to the weather.

The worst part of this weather has to be dealing with car issues. Whether it is traffic or your car just not starting, this weather causes issues. Which brings me to Zack, who as you all remember played a funny joke on me with the lottery tickets. I told Zack karma would come back to get him and guess what, it did.

His car is officially dead, gone and not coming back anytime soon. Evan (Smotrycz) is part of the issue because he apparently left Zack's lights on when moving his car earlier in the week. And for the last two weeks, Zack's car has been dying periodically. You can always tell when Zack's car isn't working properly because the doors are being slammed and horns are being honked.

Well after dinner tonight, his car died and could not be re-charged. Jordan (Morgan) came to the rescue it and gave it a jump, but Zack had to put his car in neutral at every stoplight and barely made it into our garage. I told Zack I wouldn't have to get him back, karma did its job.

Hope to see everyone at the game tonight as we play a very talented and athletic team from N.C. Central. Should be a good one!

BIG WIN, DANCING WITH STARS AND FANTASY BREAKDOWNS

Hey everyone! Hope you all are doing well because I know our team is.

The Oakland game was a very big win as we continue to protect our home court. Oakland is a very good team and they have played an incredibly hard schedule with games against Purdue, Michigan State, Illinois and Tennessee – all on the road! We came fired up right from the start and everyone on our team knew it was going to be a special day.

A lot of credit has to go to our big guys for the job they did on Keith Benson. Jordan (Morgan), Blake (McLimans) and Jon (Horford) all really showed they can compete with one of the best big guys in the country and controlled the inside. That was a huge key to the game and we worked on all week being the aggressor and making the first contact in the post

Another key to our game was the fans. We had a great crowd on Saturday and it really does make a huge difference. The Maize Rage is one of the best student sections in college sports and they definitely impact the visiting team. I have had some friends on opposing teams admit they lost focus a couple times because of different chants our Maize Rage came up with. Every single player on our team really appreciates them showing up and supporting us every game and we hope the numbers keep increasing with Big Ten play starting soon.

The day after the Oakland game we had a light practice which included film and weight lifting. While we were lifting weights, I saw something that I have wanted to blog about for a while, but I kept forgetting.

It is … The way in which Corey (Person) and Eso (Akunne) are always dancing – if you even want to call it that. Their lockers are next to each other and they always just start dancing. I am not sure how to describe it besides it is hard to watch and you just feel bad.

It would be one thing if they had a rhythm or flow, but it is just a lot of body parts swinging around. Today was another perfect example. We are all cleaning the weight room and I look to the left and Eso and Corey are "breaking it down."

When this happens you find the team just staring and shaking their heads. If you are lucky, you might catch them showing off their swag before a game.

On a way more important note, right now is a very intense time in our house. All of the freshmen are over and we are watching NFL football because it is fantasy football playoffs time. None of us play for money because that is against the NCAA rules, but we all need to win for pride reasons. Mine and (Zack) Novak's teams are in the semifinals, Stu's (Douglass) team is out and Evan (Smotrycz) claims to have made the playoffs of his league.

I have always said fantasy football is a lot of luck, but if Novak loses this week he can only blame himself. He had Vincent Jackson, Austin Collie and Ronnie Brown all sitting on his bench this weekend. Funny thing is they all scored touchdowns. Every time there was a game break, it was guaranteed Novak was upset he didn't start someone.

With that I hope everyone has a safe and wonderful holiday break

12/27/2010

THE BIG TRIP, THE NASCAR MOVES, THE GIFT COLLECTOR

Happy Holidays to everyone! I hope you all had a great and relaxing holiday weekend. We were back at work today getting ready for the start of Big Ten season and our huge game against Purdue Tuesday afternoon.

Before we can talk about Purdue, we must first talk about my first Christmas. I had seen all the movies and heard all the songs about what Christmas was supposed to be, but never first hand had I ever experienced a true Christmas. Normally I went with my family to a movie and ate some Chinese food.

Well this would all change because I was lucky enough to spend the weekend in Chesterton, Indiana, with Zack Novak.

So after our win against Bryant, we hit the road and began the drive to the great city of Chesterton. You see for almost two years I have heard story after story about "cheese town" and all the mythical things that happen there.

So just some important facts everyone knows before we break down my visit. The MTV show MADE has made two episodes at Chesterton High, but Zack did not appear in either. It takes 25 minutes to drive from one side of Chesterton to the other. Lastly it doesn't have one truck stop, but two in fact.

I woke up Friday morning and Zack told me he was going to take me to his favorite breakfast spot in Chesterton. I was starving and very excited to enjoy an omelet and maybe some pancakes. After driving for a little, we pulled into a little restaurant that I could have sworn was in Spanish.

I thought maybe we were turning around or something was wrong with the car since there always seems to be an issue, but no we were eating Mexican food at 10:30 in the morning. I really was not feeling this, first off I don't like Mexican food and second I really dislike it at 10:30 in the morning, But Zack said this was tradition and sure enough I ate chips and Salsa for breakfast that morning. I can assure you the service was great since there were only two people in the entire place.

After breakfast, Zack had to do some last minute shopping so we continued on our way to the outlet mall. Novak is very big on the coupon book at outlet malls. He must have it to see all the great deals and what different stores have to offer.

So the night before Zack signed up for the premium package at the Michigan City Outlet and was very happy with himself he already had it taken care of. Well we showed up Friday and sure enough we didn't get any coupon book. Some very old lady working behind the desk, made it very clear these were PRIME outlets and she kept repeating it over and over to Zack. One big thing I took away from this trip was Michigan City has a prime outlet mall and not a premium outlet mall, however I still have no idea what the difference is.

Remember when I said Zack always has car trouble?

Well his bad luck struck again as we were leaving his friends house. Some lady cut us off and Novak pulling his best Jeff Gordon impression hit the brakes very hard. He did save my life probably, but he ruined his brakes in the process as they were shot. I really couldn't stop laughing as we just got the car back from the shop last week and already it's undrivable again.

But the best part of the story is the car we returned to campus in. Zack had to borrow his brother's car who attended Purdue. Well this car has a big Purdue decal on the license plate, which wouldn't be a big deal but we play them in a day. So if any fan see's Zack get out of a car with Purdue stuff on it, trust me he hasn't gone crazy and it is only a temporary move. Actually I probably shouldn't promise that because the Zack's real car only can last a week without some other issue arising.

Finally we made it to Christmas Eve dinner at Zack's house. I got to meet his entire family and they were all very nice to me. His mom is a great cook and I've never seen so many appetizers before. However everyone was very hesitant to tell me anything in great detail for one big reason – My Blog.

I can't tell you how many comments I got from people saying "be careful what you tell him, it might end up in the blog" or "that's the blog guy, don't tell him that." They were all joking of course, but Novak swears that everyone was on their best behavior because of me being there.

For almost a month now I have heard nothing but how many gifts I got for Hanukkah. Well multiply whatever I got by five and that is what Christmas is like. I have never seen anything like it. Maybe because they are all opened at one time, but I swear I spent a whole day watching Zack open gifts.

My job for the weekend was to be Zack's personal gift holder and this was a true workout. I can tell you anyone who celebrates both Hanukkah and Christmas; they are just one of the luckiest people in the world.

That's all for now and I promise to answer questions next time, I just got behind. See you all Tuesday as I hear it is close to a sell out.

Q&A TIME, THE WIZARD AND B-SCHOOL FOOD

Hey everyone! Before I begin, I wanted to wish you and your family all a Happy New Year as 2011 quickly approaches. As for us, we will be ringing in the year by seeing a team movie tomorrow night as the clock approaches midnight.

Okay, I know what happened? All I can say is the Purdue game was very tough in that we gave them such a big early lead and then battled back so hard only to lose it late in the second half. The good thing is we have had a couple days of really good practice to fix some things we needed to address from the game. We keep learning and the film was very valuable.

We are finishing up the last little break between games before it gets crazy with travel and games twice a week. Ah Big Ten season. We can get into a routine where you have two days to prepare for a team, there is no looking back now. But hey, this is the best part of the season!

Now to some of your great questions I promised to get to.

FROM KRISTIE

Enjoy your blog I am a faithful reader. My question is ... who is the smartest student on the team? My guess is Corey Person.

This is a very controversial question Kristie. First off I'm not sure if you're Corey's sister or cousin, but you would have a lot of people nominate themselves for the smartest player on the team. Jordan Morgan is in the engineering school, which is no joke, so he has to be nominated, Zack Novak and Matt Vogrich are both in the business school and that is one of the top schools in the country.

On a side note, the best part of our business school has to be the cafeteria. I'm telling you this place has everything and it is fresh. I don't want to be in the school, just access to the food area.

Okay, I am back. As long as no math is involved, I will nominate myself as well for this honor as well. Corey probably ranks up there as well, but he doesn't get to class on time enough!

FROM DREW

1) In practice, what percentage of the time do you personally spend playing point guard, and what percentage at shooting guard?

I would say I play point guard and shooting guard an equal amount in practice. Coach Beilein's offense is unique in that both guard spots are the exact same, so whoever gets the ball can push it themselves.

2) In practice, does the team have different drills for the big guys and the guards? If so, what about the players who are medium-sized, like Evan Smotrycz and Colton Christian?

Yes, Drew we spend a lot of time working on skills with our different coaches. I would probably say 20 minutes of practice is devoted to just this. Coach (Bacari) Alexander works with the bigs, Coach (LaVall) Jordan with the guards and Coach (Jeff) Meyer with the wings. So players like Evan and Colton can work with Coach Meyer.

Speaking of Coach Meyer, my new nickname for him is the "wizard." No one is better at coming up with plays and little quirks to them than Coach Meyer. We always see him drawing things up and trying them out to see if they will work. He is truly a great coach!

FROM CHAMPSWEST@COMCAST.NET

What is the biggest adjustment or hardest thing for a freshman player to cope with?

Good question. I think the hardest think for freshmen is time management. We have very busy schedules and, if you don't manage your time right, you will fall behind in basketball but more importantly school. We don't have much time to sit back and relax, that time must go into studying.

When going through the handshake line after games, does anyone ever say anything other than "good game" or "good luck?"

No, most of the time guys are just saying good game and good luck the rest of the way. I'm sure during the game things are said in the heat of battle, but the officials really try and make sure it is all kept very clean. With all of our games being on TV, anything you say will be caught.

Lastly, I need to give a shout out to our great managers specifically John Adler and Daniel Pinedo. People don't realize how much work they put in and how important they are to the program. They work over 60 hour weeks and don't get any reward from it. As players we probably don't appreciate them enough, but John and Dan, you guys are the best and deep down all 15 players know how hard you work for us.

Again Happy New Year everyone!!

1/7/2011
EARLY RISING, WATCH FOR THESE TWO AND SOCIAL MEDIA

What's up everyone? We got back to Ann Arbor around 2:30 a.m. after our quick flight in from Madison. What takes a long time is actually de-icing the plane and getting it ready to fly. But I will say this, it was nice seeing Darius at 9:30 a.m. this morning for our movement science class. Both of us were wide awake.

Last night's game reminded me a lot of our trip last year to Wisconsin. We played a great first half and then in the second half they just pulled away. You have to give the Badgers credit; they shot almost 50 percent from three-point range and both their four and five men shoot over 40 percent from three point range on the year. I'm not sure anyone else in the country has that. We also knew Wisconsin would really try to slow down the game and take about 30 seconds off the shot clock on each possession. It turned out to be the least amount of possessions we had in a game all year, which definitely favors them.

On our end, it is great to see Tim (Hardaway Jr.) taking the ball to the basket. T-Hard is such a great athlete and has the ability to get in the lane and make plays. I always try and tell him to get some easy baskets first and then those three-pointers you take seem a lot easier to make. He is starting to do this more and more in practice, and I think you will see it transfer over in the game.

Another player who is really impressing me is Colton (Christian). While you all may not be seeing it in the games, Colton is really playing well in practice. He has worked tirelessly with the shot doctor (Coach Beilein) and now is becoming a really good shooter. Almost every day before practice, Colton is out there shooting on the gun and getting better. With the athlete he is already, if Colton can knock down shots, everyone better watch out.

Now back to my guy T-Hard. This was a huge week in Tim's life because he finally got a Twitter account. What makes this earth-shattering news is that all year Tim has hated even the mention of Twitter. He swore he would never ever get one, but suddenly Tim had a change of heart and now is addicted.

For example, on the bus, Tim was sitting next to Matt (Vogrich) and instead of just asking him for a movie, he tweeted it to him. Tim is really getting the hang of it. So now for those of you who are keeping track, those of us who have a twitter are Evan (Smotrycz) (@evanMsmotrycz), Tim (@t_hard10), Matt (@MattVogrich13), Zack (@novak3159), Darius (@Dariusmorris4) and myself (@Jbart20).

Now for a funny note on Evan. Just before the national anthem, the Kohl Center was silent and some student yelled out "hey 23, I can't even pronounce your last name" and then he really butchered it. It got a lot of smiles on our team because everyone messes up Evan's last name and the entire side of the arena could hear him saying this.

The schedule doesn't get any easier coming up, as Kansas and Ohio State come into town. But we wouldn't want it any other way, as we know if we want to obtain our goal of getting to the NCAA tournament, we must beat good teams at home. I hope to see you all at the games this week and we should have some great crowds.

PLAYOFFS, GOTTA BE THE SHOES, CAN I DUNK? YEP

What's up everyone! Wow, what a game!

Everyone got their money's worth as they saw two teams leave it all on the court the other day. I think people walked away from the Kansas game knowing we are close to becoming a really good team, and there are just some tweaks we have to make to beat great teams like the Jayhawks.

After such a slow start – where it looked like we might not score 40 points – we really got it going. The best part is we have another chance to knock off a top three team when No. 2 Ohio State comes to town. Nothing more needs to be said.

There is definitely some tension on our team right now with the NFL playoffs going on. You have Coach Meyer and Stu (Douglass) who are hard core Colts fans; Colton (Christian) who now sports Seahawks colors; (Zack) Novak lives and dies by the Packers and (Matt) Vogrich swears by his Bears.

Matt actually told me he believes when he watches the Bears this year it brings them good luck, and they have never lost when he watches the game. I said nothing in response.

Novak is what I call an NFC North fan. He loves Brett Favre more than life itself and is a huge Packers fan, but last week he admitted he still questioned whether or not he should be a Bears fan. He is just confused.

Then you have Colton, who all year kept quiet about his 7-9 Seahawks – the worst team to ever make the playoffs. Then all the sudden on Saturday he starts texting me like he has been there all year. Really?

Lastly, the Colt fans, you can look forward to next year and hope your special teams improve. Small side note – We also have a lot of Lions fans, particularly Jordan (Morgan), but I'll leave him alone because he has taken enough abuse and they won two road games.

I have received a ton of comments about our new team shoes. Yes, they are sweet being in Maize and Blue, but they are the same shoe we have been wearing all year just in different colors. So for those who wanted to know, they are Derrick Rose's new shoes and are great.

This allows me to bring up the great Bob Bland. Bob is our equipment manager who has been around Michigan athletics for a long, long time. Bob is the guy who brings out the chairs during timeouts, or picks up the tee after the kickoff on football games. No one on our team watches the kickoffs anymore; just how fast Bob can run on and off the field. You would be surprised.

One of the really cool things I get to do as a Michigan basketball player is work with kids on their games. The Little Dribbler program has started again, and we get to work with 100 kids who love being part of Michigan athletics.

It is great seeing how excited they are to learn the game and just play on the Crisler Arena floor. The question they all ask is "Can you dunk?" or "Will you dunk?" The answer is always, "Yes I can dunk, but I'm too stiff to dunk." So to Paul and all the other kids, maybe next time I'll show off my dunking game. You never know when you might get a "shout out" in the blog.

Lastly, I hope everyone has been paying attention to Manny Harris, as he is putting up great numbers in Cleveland. It is really cool to see a former teammate who is such a good guy living out his dream. All the hard work really paid off for him.

We had a great crowd at Kansas and we look forward to seeing even more Wolverine fans against Ohio State! Thanks for all your support and we will see you Wednesday! Go Blue!

ON THE ROAD, PRECISION AND FAMILY

One of the best feelings in college basketball is getting a road win. They don't come very often and when you can celebrate in the opponent's locker room after the game – well, it just doesn't get any better.

That being said, a tough loss like the one we had the other night at Northwestern is as rough as it gets. You prepare so hard, spend hours upon hours meeting about the game plan, but in the end, it just ends with a loss. Then after the game you realize it is midnight already in Michigan and four hours later you close your eyes finally going to sleep at 4 a.m. It doesn't help having a quiz in movement science five hours later.

Northwestern is the type of team you can prepare for as much as you want, but you never get used to its style. The Princeton offense is special in that no one else runs anything like it, but it can be so effective. They do a great job of cutting hard every possession, and they surround the court with shooters. Our scout team spends extra time just trying to get their plays down because they are so different.

Another thing that sets Northwestern apart is its fans. The Big Ten has the best fans of anyone in the country. From the Maize Rage, to the Orange Crush, everywhere you go you know it will be loud. Well the Wildcat fans are the same but they throw in a little twist.

While I was warming up, about an hour before the tip, about half of their students had books and notebooks open. I had to rub my eyes to make sure I wasn't seeing things, but sure enough they were studying before the game. There is a reason they attend Northwestern.

Lastly, playing Northwestern means I get to play at home. It is amazing how many Michigan fans attend the game. It is awesome to see so many people wearing Maize and Blue and cheering for the Wolverines.

For Matt (Vogrich) and me, it is really special getting to play in front of all our family and friends. It is very humbling to think so many people want to come and see you. From our high school coaches to grandparents and friends, it is a feeling hard to explain.

With that, I hope to see many of you on Saturday against Minnesota. It feels like forever since we played at Crisler and I know we can't wait to see our fans.

Until then, Go Blue!

1/26/2011

PETE'S HAIRCUT, STUCK IN LIMBO, THE CONTEST & I NEED A HAIRCUT

What's up everybody!

Another top ranked opponent, and very close loss at home. We got off to a great start against Minnesota, but their size and rebounding really hurt us down the stretch. We just have to keep working, and I know it will pay off.

The best part about playing in the Big Ten is every game you have a chance to beat a really good opponent. We have a job to go into East Lansing on Thursday and start a new streak. There will be no better feeling then leaving the Breslin Center with a win.

I have students ask me all the time, "Do you guys watch the games you play?" I tell all of them the same thing. We watch more film than any team in the country, and our coaches break down more film than any coaching staff in the country.

From Coach Beilein to all three assistants, they spend their lives finding ways for us to be better. We have a great video equipment guy in Pete (make sure you check out his new haircut), who cuts every game into clips depending on position. We pretty much have it all covered.

How about this ...

Some people on our team often suggest I struggle with simple tasks that the normal human beings find pretty easy. I tend to believe it is extremely over exaggerated, but yesterday, a pretty good example did show up. My car needed a wash really bad, so after practice I headed down to the gas station.

After pulling my car in and all the soap being poured over my car, the light was still red, meaning don't move. So I did just that and stayed in my spot. (Zack) Novak and company insist the light had to be green, but I'll stick to my story of a red light.

Anyway to make a long story short, as I was pulling my car out, the doors closed and half my car was stuck half inside and half outside. I was convinced my life was going to end as either the doors were going to close on me or something would blow up.

Thank god for Sammy, the gas station attendant, as he came in and saved the day. Without him, I may not be writing this blog right now.

Next up ...

As the end of January rolls around, it means one thing. There is a good chance Jordan (Morgan) will be getting a new phone. Jordan loves accessories and he really loves phones. Since I've met him, I'd say he has had five or six different phones. Some people like (Matt) Vogrich always break their phone and need a new one, but Jordan doesn't ever break it, he just gets sick of it.

The best story with Jordan and phones happened last year. I walked into the locker room one day and there was Jordan intently typing a paper on the computer. I figured he had some big assignment and was just trying to finish it up. Wrong!

Jordan was entering a contest to win a free phone. He had everyone on our team read it and give him advice. My advice was this: 10 people win and thousands upon thousands enter the contest. You are wasting your time. He assured me I was wrong and he would win the free phone. Guess who ended up being right. (It wasn't him).

Hopefully we can get a great win Thursday.

BIG WIN, COACH SINGING, TRIPLE-DOUBLE & YOUR QUESTIONS

Well just a little has changed since I last blogged. We happened to beat some team in East Lansing that a lot of people seem to care a great deal about. All I have to say is ...

What a game!

It was crazy to be a part of and I really wish all of our fans could have been in the locker room after the game. We went into a very hostile environment where the fans know way more about you then they should and when we left all I heard was a lot of silence.

As a player, that is the best feeling when you see the fans with their hands over their heads not saying a word. We have worked so hard and everyone wanted to win that game, not just for all 15 players on our team but also all of our great fans. We talked all week about how Maize and Blue nation needed this win and we got it for all of you.

I was really happy for Coach Beilein. He has worked so hard and we could all tell how much this win meant for him. He was even a little speechless after the game, but we got him to sing "The Victors," which was a great moment.

For me, if someone asked me what the best part of my basketball career has been since I arrived on campus – it would be it seeing Coach singing "The Victors" at Michigan State.

We then beat Iowa at home, a game in which we showed off our great passing and shooting. It also helps when Darius (Morris) plays like Magic Johnson and picks up a triple-double. It was like a replay over and over, Darius to Jordan for a dunk, Darius to Tim for a three, back to Jordan for a dunk and then to Evan for a three.

I heard the little dribblers put in a terrific show at halftime of the game, so congrats to all of them for a job well done. We will see you on Friday for the pizza party.

Lastly, before I try to answer as many questions as possible, we get to play our other rival school in Ohio this week.

As I told my teammates, does it get any better than going to play the undefeated No. 1 team in the country on the road who happens to be your rival? This is what we all dreamed about growing up and now we have to go live it out Thursday night!

Onto your questions... sorry it has taken so long

***

» From Brad

Who chooses what color uniforms you are going to where and how often do you get new shoes?

Can you get a different color/style before every game?

ANSWER: Great question Brad. I get this question a lot. Our equipment manager Bob Bland chooses what uniforms we wear, but we get some say on what color. We can't wear blue at home or white on the road, but maize can be worn all the time. So depending on the color of jersey we then pick what color shoes. We have maize, black and white shoes and multiple versions of each color. I know we are very spoiled, but we all appreciate how much adidas gives us. So yes the styles do change from game to game, if I had to guess you will see maize on Thursday.

***

» From Drew

Are you guys coached to try to put offensive rebounds back up, or is it an individual decision? I've noticed that most of the time the rebounder puts it right back up, instead of kicking it back out to run the offense again.

We are coached, if you can score right away, then go back up with it, but we have such great shooters that if you are double-teamed kick it out and we can get a great shot from your rebound. A lot of people don't realize one of the best ways to get an open three is off a missed shot. Coach Alexander has a done a great job helping everyone with rebounding and how to get the ball back out.

Do the coaches emphasize following your shot, especially on a long three-pointer? I've noticed that some of the U-M players are better at it than others. Are there some cases where the shooter is supposed to get back on defense instead of following his shot?

ANSWER: It depends on who shoots the shot. If a guard shoots the ball, we need him to get back on defense to prevent transition, but if a wing or big guy shoots the ball, he better go after that rebound because that is his job.

Does Zack Novak hustle as hard in practice as he does in games? He has the most hustle of any player I've seen in the last 35 years, except maybe Thad Garner (U-M 1978-1982).

ANSWER: Novak only knows one way to play and that is hard. Every day no matter game or practice he goes all out and it is contagious to our team. When you see one of your best players and captains going that hard, it sets a tone and message that this is how we do things here at Michigan.

How many different pairs of shoes do you guys have? Do you like the fancy maize-and-blue ones?

ANSWER: Yes, we have a lot of shoes and the fancy new maize ones are my favorite. ***

» From Joseph

This probably seems like a joke, but I don't mean it to be a joke. It's my understanding that your father is a sports agent. As I know it, the NCAA generally frowns on contact between student-athletes and sports agents. To ask my question in a joking way, are you allowed to talk to your dad? In a more serious way, does the NCAA have exceptions for your situation? Do they just have a VP of Common Sense (copyright Bill Simmons) who recognizes that it would be absurd to punish you? And what if you bring friends home for Hanukkah, like Novak took you home for Christmas? Would your athlete friends be allowed to talk to your dad?

ANSWER: Interesting question Joseph. I talk to my dad everyday so I sure hope that isn't breaking any NCAA rules. I guess when I go to the NBA I will already have an agent picked out. I think the NCAA would have some common sense, but yes my teammates talk to my dad just like he was some sort of normal guy with a normal job. It isn't a big deal and I don't think ever will be.

***

» From Katie

Hi, I'm a high school senior, and I will most likely be attending the University of Michigan next year. My question is... what has been your best Michigan memory, sports related or not?

ANSWER: I already told you my best basketball memory, with Coach B singing The Victors at MSU. My best non-related sports memory has to be just meeting all the alumni and fans who love Michigan. Whether it is walking around campus or just sitting in the hotel lobby on the road, it is great to see so many people bleed Maize and Blue. Coming into college I didn't realize much people love Michigan; I sure do now.

***

» From Brent

What kind of ball-handling drills do you guys do during practice and what is the best way I can develop my left-handed dribble?

ANSWER: We have some great ball-handling drills. I'm a big fan of dribble around cones and simulating them as defenders. To work on your left hand, just pound the ball with your left hand and dribble all around the court with just that hand. The thing with ball handling is, if you spend 15 minutes everyday working on it, you will see dramatic improvements really fast. You just got to be consistent with it.

Also, how excited is the team about the new basketball specific practice facility being built next door? What will this allow you guys to do differently next year?

ANSWER: I can't wait. We our going to have our own state-of-the-art, well, everything. From a new locker room to swimming pools to a new weight room to just about anything you could imagine will be in the new facility. It will allow us to practice whenever we want because there will no longer be conflicts with the women's team and 24-hour access to shoot on our own. It is really coming along nicely now. Actually resembles a building and not just a hole in the ground.

***

» From Laura

Two questions for you... Lately the entertainment has been expanded from just halftime to also during the longer media timeouts. Do the players usually have any idea what's going on? Are you distracted or amused? Second, how aware are the players on the bench and the players on the court aware of what the crowd is chanting and shouting?

ANSWERS: We can't really pay attention to the court during timeouts because we must be focused in the timeout. I'm sure some guys take a peek to see what is happening when the crowd is going crazy, but overall we are all focused on the game. We can hear people chanting, but a lot of the time it is hard to make out what they are exactly saying.

***

» From Lawrence

Do the players get the same educational assistance in the offseason as during the season?

ANSWER: Yes, as long as we are in school, we have great academic assistance. Tommy Jones is our academic counselor and he provides everything from tutors to book to scheduling appointments. We are very lucky to have him and he makes a huge difference. Athletes even have their own study center that really helps us out with everything being centrally located.

***

» From Tommy

QUESTION: Hey Josh, Why does Smotrycz wear what looks like pads on his legs?

ANSWER: I think Evan is going for the Walt Williams look if any of you know who that is. In all seriousness, he has some serious bruised knees and those pads prevent him from making them any worse. At the same time, I make fun of him all the time for looking like a ballerina.

I almost forgot, but thanks to everyone who told me where to get a haircut. From the media to fans to even some players I got a ton of suggestions.

Some gave me places in A2, others in Ypsilanti, a place in Ohio and some people even offered to come to my house and cut it themselves. I even got a girl saying if I took her out on a date she would give me a haircut for free. I have a tough choice to make.

2/10/2011

TEAM PLAY, ANOTHER BIG GAME AND THANK YOU PACKERS

What's up everyone! It's great to be a Michigan Wolverine these days!

Anytime you win four out of five in the Big Ten, you know you are doing something right. I love the way our team is playing – everyone is making the extra pass and everyone is playing total team basketball. It helps too when Jordan Morgan finishes like Dwight Howard down low. Did you see his performance against Northwestern? He just keeps getting better and better, but what many don't realize his best play of that game came on the defensive end – that is how we need to keep playing.

We all know our offense can play with almost anyone, but when we play great team defense we know we can play with anyone. Northwestern has such a unique offense, that it took a great couple days of practice to get prepared. Coach Jordan did a really good job with the scouting report and we changed some things up from the last time we played them. It worked really well in the first half, and then in the second it was an offensive battle. I'm just happy we won!

Now we go into another big game against Indiana, who beat us in Bloomington in mid-January. We all want payback on the Hoosiers and I know we will be ready. They present different challenges that we will work on in practice tomorrow and implement Saturday afternoon. We need all our Wolverine fans to be in attendance Saturday, it is that time of the year where you make that NCAA tournament run.

Switching gears...

Thankfully the Packers won the Super Bowl!!

I was cheering for the Steelers and Rashard Mendenhall, but as the game went on, I realized for my safety it was very important the Packers won. (Zack) Novak was close to breaking the TV after every dropped pass and at that point I took cover after every play. I knew I had to re-think my allegiance.

He was rocking his Rodgers jersey and as soon as the game ended, he ordered the Super Bowl hat and shirt. He couldn't stop smiling and I figured after all he went through this year with his childhood idol in Brett Favre, he could use a big win like this.

That's the kind of roommate I am. Make no mistake, if the Steelers had won, I would not be able to write this blog right now.

With that I have to go study for a test, but next time I'll write an extra long blog.

See you on Saturday.

2/21/2011

CHANGING IT UP AND RORY ROCKS!

Hey everyone?

What a week, first we almost make a miracle shot at the buzzer against Illinois and then we pull out a great win at Iowa on the road. It was a crazy game in which the big three – D-Mo, J-Mo and Tim – played great and we got a huge road win.

Now we come back home and we need the biggest home court advantage ever against Wisconsin. We have the greatest fans and I'm sure everyone will see it for themselves on Wednesday.

Our coaches are all about having a set routine and making sure you stick to it. Tim for example likes taking extremely long naps, to the point you really can't consider it a nap, more of a second bed time. Jordan and Darius blast the music as loud as possible so it resonates on the entire hotel floor, while, (Zack) Novak foam rolls his body.

However, at Iowa we switched it up a bit and took a long walk outside. Yes, that's right the Michigan basketball team took a walk and observed the beautiful nature of Iowa. It was a way for us to get some fresh air and not sit around the hotel all morning. All I know is we won, so if you see us walking outside Crisler or on the road don't think we are crazy, it is just a new routine.

If you asked anyone on our team besides playing games, what the best part of being a Michigan basketball player is, the answer would be being a part of Michigan from the Heart.

Michigan from the Heart is a program where student-athletes get to visit patients at Mott's Children's hospital and meet with them for a while. While patients say all the time how grateful they are we stopped by, it is a huge honor for us to meet these kids and hopefully make them smile. We all feel so lucky to represent such a prestigious university and be part of a tremendous program.

The other day we all met a kid named Rory who is battling cancer for the second time. He may be the bravest person I have ever met and the whole time he had a smile on his face. We talked for awhile and then I got him an autographed shoe from our team.

He loved it but from my perspective, and Jordan Morgan's, it wasn't anywhere near enough to show how much we appreciate him being there as a fan. Rory gave us all yellow wrist bands that say "Rory Rocks, We Believe" and I can tell you, Rory, the entire Michigan team believes with you and is rocking the yellow wrist band wherever we go.

So Rory, if we can do anything for you and anyone else from Michigan from the Heart please let us know and we will do our best because you are a big part of our basketball family.

I will see you on Wednesday. Go Blue!

3/17/2011

WHAT A GAME, JUSTIN BIEBER AND MONOPOLY!

What a day!

I'm pretty sure everyone is rocking their Maize and Blue today and we all have good reason to. The atmosphere at Crisler on Saturday was electric, the best I have seen in the two years I have been here. The Maize pom-poms made it seem like the place was rocking back and forth. As a visitor, I would not want to play at Crisler Arena right now.

For the first time in a very long time, we had a full week to prepare for an opponent. It was a big advantage to be able to rest up and game plan while the other team has to play during the week. When you give coaches like John Beilein and his staff a full week, they are going to install a top-notch game plan. I can recall a couple times this year where we played a team after they had a full week to prepare and it makes a difference – remember Indiana on the road?

I have to give a lot of credit to Stu (Douglass) and Darius (Morris) as they both battled sickness and lead us to victory. They didn't complain, they just kept fighting and it paid off big time. Also, Evan (Smotrycz) was huge yesterday in giving us a big spark off the bench. There are not a lot of 6-10 people who are as versatile as Evan. To think he is only a freshman and can step in and play like that is a scary thought for opponents.

After the game yesterday, I had tons of people ask what's the big difference between now and two months ago when you were last in the big ten. The truth is all the small things are making a huge difference.

There is such a small line between winning and losing that a play here or there makes all the difference in the world. We just learned to value every possession and as coach Jordan always preaches, making winning plays. We started making the extra pass, taking charges and believing in the offense even when the shot clock is at 10. You are seeing a young team mature and learn how to win.

When you play basketball at the University of Michigan, you spend every possible break in Ann Arbor with no one else around. So we have a lot of time to try and find things to do. We went to two movies including the Justin Bieber movie and we definitely now have some big Bieber fans on our team.

It really is an amazing story. The biggest thing that happened this break was Monopoly. I bought the electronic version and we pretty much have had team tournaments every night since. Of course every member of our team proclaims to be undefeated and know some secret to the game no one else knows.

Once we started playing however, it was clear certain people didn't belong. Let's just say it is a good thing Evan and Tim (Hardaway Jr.) are really good at basketball because Monopoly just isn't their game. Zack (Novak) has banned Evan from playing because he made a bad trade with me and I went on to dominate the board. Apparently the next day Evan was practicing on the computer in preparation for the next day. He performed much better at the team hotel on Friday night.

That's all for oow and I hope to see a ton of Michigan fans in Indy. We need all of you there to join the Maize Rage in representing the Maize and Blue in Indy.

OH AND A BIG SHOUT OUT TO RORY!!! Rory was at our game against Michigan State and he was a good luck charm so we trying to get him to practice this week We all believe Rory! I also wanted to give a shout out to our student trainer, Brad, and the video he made... check it out here! Go Blue!

STUDY HALL, PRACTICE, MOVEMENT SCIENCE

What's up everyone?

I'm writing to you from the Charlotte room in the beautiful Hilton as we are conducting our study hall. Not too many people are thrilled with having to do work with the game being hours away but it is part of being a student-athlete.

Today has been a really busy day. We woke up around 9 a.m. and had a film session. As Jon Horford, would say "a quality session of watching film." Then we went on to practice at a school about 20 minutes away.

This practice was closed to the media so we were able to put in our final game plan for tomorrow. Right after that we continued on to Time Warner Cable Arena for our open practice.

First we had a media session and this is when you can tell you aren't playing any regular season game with the amount of cameras in attendance. So many of us are just trying to take in the moment of actually getting to play in the NCAA tournament. We have been talking about this since we were little kids and only dreamt one day it would come to fruition. We know tomorrow morning we can't be wide eyed anymore because there is business to take care off.

Practice went very well. I just hope the fans didn't show up to see a dunk contest because we did no dunking. Instead we worked on what has made us successful this year, which included shooting drills, lay-ups and pivoting drills. You would think I was talking about a sixth grade school team, but what makes Coach Beilein so highly regarded is how skilled his players are and the reason why is because we all practice things most say is simple.

The rest of the day we watched the games which included Matt Howard of Butler hitting a game winning shot and of course Morehead State beats Louisville. I'm sure all of you guys had that one in your brackets.

The rest of the week I will try and provide updates on what we are doing, that may be shorter blog installments.

You can also follow me on twitter (@Jbart20) as I will try and give updates on our daily occurrences.

Now Darius and I have to study for Movement Science 110.

Be back soon! Go Blue!

HUGE DAY, LOTS OF THANKS AND TIGER BLOOD

What's up everyone?

What a day!

What a win!

I don't even really know to start. We just had such a great team effort out there against Tennessee and had so much fun in the process. From Zack (Novak) hitting three after three; to Matt (Vogrich) taking over the game; to Stu (Douglass) dunking on someone. Not a bad afternoon of basketball.

Our fans have been great so far in Charlotte. From leaving the hotel with the band playing the fight song and even arriving at the stadium with the sirens from the police escort blaring wherever we go the Maize and Blue following has been special. I even had a couple fans yell at me as I ran onto the court today saying "today may be the best blog ever" and they were right on. Shout out to them!

Tomorrow is a new day which means we need to refocus and get ready for Duke. We will watch a ton of film have a short 90 minute practice and rest up for what should be a great game Sunday afternoon. I hear Ann Arbor is buzzing over the game and we can't wait to get out there and represent Michigan.

I have to give one huge shout out to our band. Coach Beilein says they are the best in the country and I have to agree. They are always creating great energy for the team and we appreciate all they do.

One quick story about number zero. He is a really, really big fan of Charlie Sheen and his favorite TV show is Two and a Half Men. So when we ran onto the court and saw a picture of Novak with the writing Novak has tiger blood I knew it would make his day. Sure enough the poster is hanging up in our hotel room right now and will make the trip back to Ann Arbor with us. So, whoever made that THANKS!

I will try and write again tomorrow until then enjoy the madness of March!

REASONS TO SMILE & REASONS TO BE PROUD

As I was sitting in our locker room listening to Coach Beilein talk the day after our game against Duke, I couldn't help but think where this program stood a year ago. Because at the end of the day, all 15 of us want to leave a mark on the Michigan basketball program that will never be forgotten.

Just like Cazzie Russell and Glen Rice and most recently Travis Conlin and the Great C.J. Lee did. A year ago, people hung their heads when they talked about Michigan basketball. There was no excitement. It looked like we were going into complete rebuilding mode. It is amazing what a lot of hard work and a group of 15 teammates and four coaches can do when they only have one true goal in mind.

It wasn't easy and there where some major stumbling blocks in the way. We started the year in August with two-a-day practices in the hottest gym in America. Most teams were enjoying themselves with the summer weather lying by the pool but we just started building the foundation for a team that we knew was going to be really good. At the time no one else did.

We went to Belgium and played against four professional teams. We went 1-3 and the alarms started going off. How could a team that was supposed compete in the Big Ten not even win in Europe? But we had a great time on the trip and it was an extremely successful journey. The bonds we shared walking through Belgium and Amsterdam, seeing where Ann Frank lived and making the climb to the top of the Eiffel Tower are memories I will never forget. We will never forget and the bond of 15 young men really accelerated across the pond.

We were picked last in the Big Ten. Maybe we would get double digits win was the consensus. But we started of the year strong beating good teams like Harvard and Oakland and nearly pulling off a great wins against Syracuse, Kansas and Ohio State.

The momentum going into that Big Ten home opener was huge and a sold out Crisler Arena awaited the Boilermakers. We got off to a bad start, but managed to fight our way back into that game. A reoccurring theme some would go on to say. We lost that game and ended up starting the Big Ten season 1-6. Some around the team acted like the world was going to come to an end, but those in the locker room just kept working, even harder than ever. The coaches came to work everyday with a smile on their face and you would never know we were 1-6.

It was during that 1-6 start our point guard and head coach made statements that would change our season.

Darius Morris made a public statement we are going to win at least 20 games this year. He was dead serious and the team took on his belief. We were going to find a way to win 20 games and make the NCAA tournament.

The second moment came after our toughest loss of the season in my hometown of Chicago, coach Beilein knew we were really down, searching for answers. But he said, "this group of players will play in the NCAA tournament, it might not be this year, but you all will."

Just like in all cases this year, Coach B was right. But even he wouldn't have known that it would be this year we all made the tournament. You guys all know the story from the rest of the regular season. We went on a roll no one could ever predict. Sweeping NCAA tournament teams like Penn State and Michigan State, then getting wins over Indiana and Minnesota. We had two heartbreaking losses in there against Wisconsin and Illinois, but we bounced back and finished fourth in the best conference in the country.

None of us will ever forget Selection Sunday and just how much went into that day. The amount of shots Darius took this past summer, how hard Jordan Morgan worked to get back in game shape after two surgeries, how much better Tim Hardaway Jr. got from August to March, how Evan Smotrycz and Matt Vogrich always got up shots after practice and how our two captains Stu Douglass and Zack Novak just stayed tough all year long. I could go on forever, but I don't want to get off target.

Once you get to the round of 32, you realize just how close you are – we were just one win away from the Sweet 16. Four wins away from a title. You can taste it, but at the same time you have to focus on the moment.

We were ready for Duke. We played our hearts out and that game defined our season. Nobody is supposed to come back from 15 in the second half against Duke. We did. And we were an inch away from sending the game to overtime. But basketball can be a game of inches sometimes and that's just the way the ball rolled. We redefined what it means to be the comeback kid's. We were resilient and as so many alums have told me, we were true Wolverines all the way to the end.

The two hours after that game were as tough as you can imagine. But it really should be. When you invest as much as we did, and spent every day together for about seven months, it really, really hurts.

You hear it all the time in sports, but we felt like we were family. When a member of our team had a bad day, we all felt it the same way we all loved seeing a teammate's success. This is the reason I know we have greatness ahead of us. Not because of how talented we our on the court or how good our coaches can be at preparing us, but because we have guys who love each other, love the program and love Michigan more than anyone can imagine.

It has been an honor to write this blog. Getting to meet all the fans and read your emails has been really cool. That truly has been the best part of it was hearing what all of you had to say.

The perfect example was in the process of writing this last blog I got an email from Rory's dad who just told me Rory is cancer free after his second bout with the disease. I have been sad since yesterday, but I can't help but smile now. We all believed in Rory and he came through. I can't wait to tell all of my teammates.

I have to thanks our SID, Tom Wywrot, because he asked me about writing this blog last summer and at first I was hesitant but I couldn't be happier I did it. Maybe you will see me next year writing again.

Thanks so, so much. Go Blue!

THE 2011-12 SEASON

7/29/2011

I'M BACK, SUMMER REPORTS, CONSTRUCTION BOOTS, DUNK TANKS

What is up everyone?!

The blog is back!

I had a great four-month vacation from writing, but it is time to get back at it. It seems like yesterday I was writing on the plane back from Charlotte, N.C., about what a special season we had. Four months later, so much has changed with Michigan basketball, and at the same time, our core had become even closer.

First up, Darius Morris got drafted by his hometown Lakers. We all were so happy for him and it is almost surreal to see a teammate and good friend make it to the NBA. Darius is in a perfect spot in L.A., and we all know he will do great things there.

The next bit of big basketball news of the summer came with Tim Hardaway Jr. Tim played for Team USA this summer and was a huge part of its run to a fifth-place finish in the FIBA World Championships. He was a major contributor on both ends of the court. We even noticed that because Tim has spent the last two summers in Europe, he has a little more "Euro Swag" to him. However, I am pretty sure we don't have to worry about Tim moving across the pond any time soon as the European way and him are not exactly one. We are just happy to have him back in Ann Arbor.

Everyone asks me what's going on with the construction. Well that is the next big change in A2, as Crisler Arena and the Player Development Center are under major construction. You can see how good they are going to look when they are done. There are plenty of cool construction photos on the Michigan Basketball Facebook page. Check them out!

It seemed like the construction crew just kept digging deeper and deeper into the ground without any progress, but now the PDC looks like a real building. From all that I have heard, there will be no better basketball facility in the country.

Every week we hear something new will be added in the PDC. It has taken on mythological proportions of its own – from iPads to underwater treadmills to recently even a helicopter pad. Yes, that is what I said: a helicopter. Let's just say everything has been thrown in the rumor mill and is churning. As a team, we are all just excited to have a court to practice on.

With all the construction we have had to find different places to get ready and work out. As I have always said, what makes this place special is that all the sports here are really good at sharing without even blinking an eye. So our locker room is at the baseball facility, we lift at the wrestling center and we play basketball at the IM, the CCRB or the sports Coliseum. There will be a quiz later. The good thing about the IM is that it is literally 150 degrees in there every day so getting a good sweat is easy, just tie your shoes.

Summer basketball camps at Michigan will never change. Coach B loves having his camps and they are one of the special things the program does to reach out to kids. They have great instruction and most of the players get to coach a team.

I think Coach B just wants us to see how hard of a job he really has. Tim is very serious about his team and has a set offense. It surprisingly works. Corey (Person) lets his team "just play," which isn't surprising, and (Zack) Novak doesn't like losing (very surprising). Anyone who follows our team knows that was a joke. Really? Did you see the footage from Michigan State?

If you asked any of the kids what their favorite part of the camp was they will say the dunk tank. Travis (Conlan) and C.J. (Lee) had the brilliant idea of letting the campers throw balls at a dunk tank while we fell in the water. It feels good the first time, but after the 50th time it gets a little old.

Despite being soaked to the bone, Jordan (Morgan), Evan (Smotrycz), Novak and I just kept sitting on the ledge and falling in. It turned out to be a blast. We have the pictures to prove it.

It feels really good to be back with all of you. I am looking forward to updating you again with the ins and outs of the season. I think I will write again in a week or two.

Until next time take care and Go Blue!

SUMMER DAYS GOING FAST, THE ROOKIES AND THE LEAGUE

What's up everyone!

We are finishing the last 10 days of the summer semester and the start of the real school year is just a month away. Can you believe it? The summer has been really productive so far between weights, open gyms and, of course, classes.

This week we are doing our strength and speed testing. This means after eight weeks of working out, it is time to see how much better we have gotten. It is actually really cool because everyone on our team has made dramatic improvements.

From vertical jump to hang clean, the numbers have skyrocketed up. This is a testament to Coach Sanderson and Coach Fletcher, but also all the hard work our team has put in. Every morning at 8 a.m., we are there working our tails off and it pays off. These improvements translate on to the court in October; just wait and see!

So far, I have received a ton of questions on our four new freshmen – Trey Burke, Carlton Brundidge, Max Bielfeldt and Sai Tummala. Well, let me start by saying they have all done a great job of getting used to the "Michigan" way.

Sure there are times they all act as freshmen, but overall, they have done a great job. As teammates, I couldn't ask for anymore. Trey is an aggressive attacking point guard with a big-time jump shot. Carlton finishes as well at the basket as any small guard I have seen and has an explosive first step. Sai is a tremendous athlete who is going to really surprise some people, and Max is a skilled big man who plays his behind off. I feel very confident in saying all four will have great success before all is said and done.

This coming Thursday will be a very historic for some players on our team. It isn't a final or date night, but the first ever Michigan basketball team fantasy football draft. I must first say this league is for fun only and there are NO prizes.

Pride is on the line, along with a lot of trash talking.

I'll tell the team the consensus. Who knows, we might even do it at Buffalo Wild Wings.

I will post each player's team next week and write more often once school and workouts really get going.

That's all for now. Hope you are all as excited for the season as we are. It's going to be special.

8/25/2011

BACK TO SCHOOL, DON'T FORGET YOUR DRILLS, THE LEAGUE IS HERE!

What's up everyone? I hope you are all having a great summer. It is amazing just how fast it flies by.

A year ago today we were in Belgium practicing and play games. That trip proved to be an extremely important experience both on and off the court for us. It set up what some would say was the most exciting season of Michigan men's basketball in recent history. Now the hype for this season is outrageous. We are excited to get back and get started.

For now, the entire team has the next 10 days or so off, before we report to campus on Thursday, Sept. 1, for our first team meeting. After that we can officially start working out on the Sept. 7, which will be the first time we work with our coaches since April AND the first time we get to see what has been done to Crisler Arena. We just cannot wait. We have heard so many good things.

These workouts are all about skill work with a huge emphasis on shooting and dribbling. This is when you can really start to get into a routine and focus on the upcoming season. We all know about the drills coach Beilein has. All I can say is I continue to practice them every day!

Now as promised. The U-M League is ready!

As I have said before, there is no entry fee or prizes; this is being done for just pure fun! We had the 2011 Michigan men's basketball fantasy football draft last week. Posted below are the teams. Overall we will have a round-robin format season of competition – which I will make sure you are all updated – with the top four teams making the playoffs. Then in the end someone will be the inaugural champion!

TEAM BARTELSTEIN

Philip Rivers (SD -QB) Mario Manningham (NYG -WR) Miles Austin (Dal -WR) Adrian Peterson (Min -RB) Peyton Hillis (Cle -RB) Jimmy Graham (NO -TE) Knowshon Moreno (Den -RB) Marques Colston (NO -WR) Beanie Wells (Ari -RB) Kyle Orton (Den -QB) Tim Hightower (Was -RB) Robert Meachem (NO -WR) Lee Evans (Bal -WR) Matt Bryant (Atl -K) Pittsburgh (Defense)

The Bartelstein Analysis: I believe I have the best running back combination in the league. Also, my sleeper pick is Jimmy Graham, who will be a key target for Drew Brees. I have to have a Michigan man
in Super Mario, who is due for a big year with the departure of Steve Smith.

TEAM MORGAN

Drew Brees (NO -QB) Hakeem Nicks (NYG -WR) Brandon Marshall (Mia -WR) Steven Jackson (StL -RB) Marshawn Lynch (Sea -RB) Dallas Clark (Ind -TE) Stevie Johnson (Buf -WR) Matt Schaub (Hou -QB) Eli Manning (NYG -QB) Mike Tolbert (SD -RB) Kellen Winslow (TB -TE) Plaxico Burress (NYJ -WR) Pierre Garcon (Ind -WR) David Akers (SF -K) Detroit (Defense)

The Bartelstein Analysis: J Mo has great depth at quarterback, but you have to question his running backs. Steven Jackson peaked three years ago and Marshawn Lynch had one good run in the playoffs. J Mo for some reason is a big Plaxico fan as well.

TEAM NOVAK

Aaron Rodgers (GB -QB) Greg Jennings (GB -WR) Mike Williams (Sea -WR) Chris Johnson (Ten -RB) LeGarrette Blount (TB -RB) Jermichael Finley (GB -TE) Shonn Greene (NYJ -RB) Michael Crabtree (SF -WR) Matthew Stafford (Det -QB) Ryan Grant (GB -RB) Steve Smith (Car -WR) Chris Cooley (Was -TE) Emmanuel Sanders (Pit -WR) Mason Crosby (GB -K) New England (Defense)

The Bartelstein Analysis: Novak drafted as many Packers as possible with Rodgers, Grant, Jennings, Finley and Crosby. As much as I hate to admit it he actually has a pretty good team as long as Chris Johnson doesn't hold out all year. His sleeper pick in Shonn Greene, which is a good one. He just better hope the Packers put up some points.

TEAM MCLIMANS

Rashard Mendenhall (Pit -RB) Maurice Jones-Drew (Jac -RB) Mike Wallace (Pit -WR) Dez Bryant (Dal -WR) BenJarvus Green-Ellis (NE -RB) Roy Williams (Chi -WR) Joe Flacco (Bal -QB) Tony Gonzalez (Atl -TE) Matt Cassel (KC -QB)

C.J. Spiller (Buf -RB) Lance Moore (NO -WR) Ben Roethlisberger (Pit -QB) Stephen Gostkowski (NE -K) New York (Defense) Minnesota (Defense)

The Bartelstein Analysis: An interesting mix of talent on this team. At one point I said to Blake, "You know you have taken Steelers three out of your first four picks," and he had no idea. So I just hope I'm playing his team when the Steelers have a bye week. He had to sneak one Bills pick in there, but I guess it is hard to have many Bills players on a fantasy team since they aren't exactly the greatest show on turf.

TEAM VOGRICH

Josh Freeman (TB -QB) Dwayne Bowe (KC -WR) Vincent Jackson (SD -WR) Michael Turner (Atl -RB) Matt Forte (Chi -RB) Owen Daniels (Hou -TE) Daniel Thomas (Mia -RB) Mark Ingram (NO -RB) Joseph Addai (Ind -RB) Sidney Rice (Sea -WR) Jay Cutler (Chi -QB) Devin Hester (Chi -WR) Rob Gronkowski (NE -TE) Neil Rackers (Hou -K) San Diego (Defense)

The Bartelstein Analysis: Team Chicago. With Cutler, Hester, and Forte, Vogrich has a nice stable of Bears. I think he got a steal in Vincent Jackson because no one realizes how good he is due to the fact he held out almost all of last year. He takes a big risk with rookie running backs in Ingram and Thomas, but Matt is a fantasy football veteran.

TEAM TUMMALA

Peyton Manning (Ind -QB) Andre Johnson (Hou -WR) Santonio Holmes (NYJ -WR) Jamaal Charles (KC -RB) Ahmad Bradshaw (NYG -RB) Marcedes Lewis (Jac -TE) Anquan Boldin (Bal -WR) Jeremy Maclin (Phi -WR) Cedric Benson (Cin -RB) Ryan Fitzpatrick (Buf -QB) Mike Sims-Walker (StL -WR) Brandon Pettigrew (Det -TE) Danny Woodhead (NE -RB) Alex Henery (Phi -K) Chicago (Defense)

The Bartelstein Analysis: Sai pretty much picked the best player left on the board each time he was up. It was easy to figure out who to cross of the board. I like the Maclin pick as long as he is healthy. Andre Johnson is a beast, but he is very thin at running back and I don't think Jamaal Charles is all that he is built up to be.

TEAM SMOTRYCZ/ HARDAWAY JR.

Tom Brady (NE -QB) Reggie Wayne (Ind -WR) Jahvid Best (Det -RB) Dustin Keller (NYJ -TE) Brandon Lloyd (Den -WR) Mike Williams (TB -WR) Santana Moss (Was -WR) Braylon Edwards (SF -WR)

A.J. Green (Cin -WR) Brian Robiskie (Cle -WR) Calvin Johnson (Det -WR) Felix Jones (Dal -RB) Donovan McNabb (Min -QB) Robbie Gould (Chi -K) New Orleans (Defense)

The Bartelstein Analysis: I'm going to try and be nice, but this team just doesn't make a lot of sense. You have eight wide receivers and two running backs. Not real good balance. I see some major trades being made. However, this team does hold the rights to Randy Moss if he ever comes back. Evan made/wasted a draft pick on the rights to Randy Moss.

TEAM DUMARS

DeSean Jackson (Phi -WR) Frank Gore (SF -RB)

Chad Ochocinco (NE -WR) Pierre Thomas (NO -RB) Reggie Bush (Mia -RB) Julio Jones (Atl -WR) Sam Bradford (StL -QB) Davone Bess (Mia -WR) LaDainian Tomlinson (NYJ -RB) Michael Vick (Phi -QB) Vernon Davis (SF -TE) Nate Kaeding (SD -K) Philadelphia (Defense)

The Bartelstein Analysis: Team Dumars is all about the big play and I like it. DeSean Jackson is a highlight waiting to happen along with Vick. Reggie Bush is going to surprise people in Miami and Ochocinco will come back from the dead in New England. The real question for JD is can Vick stay healthy and can he manage a team all year long? This is Jordan's first fantasy football league.

TEAM DOUGLASS

Matt Ryan (Atl -QB) Larry Fitzgerald (Ari -WR) Wes Welker (NE -WR) Arian Foster (Hou -RB) DeAngelo Williams (Car -RB) Antonio Gates (SD -TE) Fred Jackson (Buf -RB) Percy Harvin (Min -WR) Kevin Kolb (Ari -QB) Tony Moeaki (KC -TE) Thomas Jones (KC -RB) Mike Thomas (Jac -WR) Brandon Jacobs (NYG -RB) Sebastian Janikowski (Oak -K) Green Bay (Defense)

The Bartelstein Analysis: My favorite team besides mine. Great balance and you know Larry Fiztgerald will have a huge year after getting a new QB and a nice new contract. Foster is a stud, but he lost his starting all-pro fullback. Maybe the favorite before the season starts.

TEAM BIELFELDT

Mark Sanchez (NYJ -QB) Roddy White (Atl -WR) Austin Collie (Ind -WR) Ray Rice (Bal -RB) LeSean McCoy (Phi -RB) Jason Witten (Dal -TE) Darren McFadden (Oak -RB)

Tony Romo (Dal -QB) Kenny Britt (Ten -WR) Ryan Mathews (SD -RB) Hines Ward (Pit -WR) Zach Miller (Sea -TE) Garrett Hartley (NO -K) New York (Defense) Baltimore (Defense)

The Bartelstein Analysis: I have to give Max credit, he did draft well. He is loaded in the backfield, but his big question will be can Romo have a big year? If he does, Max has as good of a team as anyone.

180 DEGREES OF CHANGE, SAD SOX AND DANCING WITH THE STARS

What's up everyone? We are officially back!

School has begun, Crisler Arena is open and most importantly, we got our new gear! Well maybe school beginning or the opening of Crisler outweighs the gear.

This past Tuesday (Sept. 6), we had our first conditioning workout with our basketball coaches present. It's been awhile since we have been all together. Later this week we will have our first individual workouts in groups of four and the cycle of a new season will be in full swing. I cannot wait!

The first thing I need to talk about is just how good Crisler Arena looks. Check out the gallery!

The sad part is nothing I say and no pictures you guys see will do justice to how good it looks. It is a complete 180. There is no college arena I have been to in my two years that looks better. The court, the railings, the seats, the lights, the floor and the scoreboard make it feel completely new.

I'm not one for hyping things up and I didn't really buy into all this Crisler hype, but trust me you guys are in for a huge surprise. If you could have seen the smile on Tim's (Hardaway Jr.) face or Corey (Person) running around the entire court you would understand just how shocked and happy everyone was.

We are just so appreciative to the university and the athletic department for doing all that they have. We all feel really lucky to be part of all of this.

Now, I must break and move onto a much less happier subject.

On Sunday, coach Meyer, Jordan (Morgan), Zack (Novak) and myself attended the White Sox/Tigers game. Zack, coach Meyer, and I are huge White Sox fans and Jordan is a real big Tigers fan. Let me backtrack just for a second so I can talk about the events of Saturday (Sept. 3). We – the White Sox that is – were beating the Tigers 8-1, a huge lead and one that should never be lost.

It was setting up for the biggest game of the year on Sunday night. Next thing I know, we are eating a team dinner at Pizza House and the score is 8-6 in the ninth. Then, I hear this yell from Travis (Conlan), coach Alexander and Jordan – three of the biggest Tiger fans you can find. I went into a complete shell and no longer ate my BBQ chicken as I was actually sick to my stomach – 9-8 final, the Sox blew it.

So now I go to the game Sunday thinking this cannot get any worse and I am just going to enjoy a nice baseball game. I was very wrong. Well, let's just say 18 Tiger runs and three White Sox errors later I wasn't really enjoying the game. It was like watching the Bad News Bears. To make matters even worse, I have to let Jordan paint my face like a Tiger because I made a bet when we were losing 5-0 that there was no way we would be down 10-0 -I clearly lost that one. The moral of the story is that it really sucked being a White Sox fan this weekend. Period.

Okay transitioning back, there is no question we have a lot of fun off the court and that sure didn't change on Monday night. We had the athletic center Welcome Back BBQ where all the athletes get together to kick off another year.

Besides the spectacular food, we had some amazing dancing by two of our freshmen – the one and only Sai (Tummala) and the great Carlton (Brundidge) were asked to break it down by our captains. Sai was supposed to do the "Dougie" and Carlton attempted to do the "Macarena." I'm not really sure how to explain what either of them actually did, but Sai contorted his body in a way I had never seen and Carlton really broke down the Macarena. (Click on the above links to see what they were really supposed to do.) All video of them has yet to be found!

It is a good thing both are really good at basketball because neither will be appearing on Dancing with Stars anytime soon.

Lastly, this weekend is the start of the Michigan Basketball fantasy football league.

This week's match-ups, which I'm sure you will hear about all week via Twitter are: Me vs. Jordan; Zack vs. Max (Bielfeldt); Blake (McLimans) vs. Jordan (Dumars), Matt (Vogrich) vs. Evan (Smotrycz) and Sai vs. Stu (Douglass).

Zack has the highest projected points and Evan has the lowest for what that is worth. We will see how it all plays out.

Until then, Go Blue! Enjoy the Under the Lights game vs. Notre Dame. It should be exciting – don't worry, I will post how that all goes.

WINNING!, THE BILLS, A REAL PRACTICE, 50-IN-5, CAN'T WAIT!

What's up everyone?

Not a bad time to be a fan of the State of Michigan. The Wolverines are now ranked No. 21 in football, the Tigers clinched the Central Division and the Lions are 2-0. I can't say I support all those teams, but I'm happy for all of you that have dealt with losing professional teams for too long. I have been spoiled in Chicago – six NBA titles and the White Sox winning the World Series in 2005.

The other very important thing about the beginning of the NFL season is the Buffalo Bills are 2-0. I have no ties to Buffalo besides the fact that Coach Beilein is a huge Bills fan. On most Sundays during the year, we have practice during the NFL games and usually don't catch any of the action.

This would all change if the Bills had a solid team because Coach B would want to watch them play and therefore practice would be later in the day. So everyone on our team – especially Matt (Vogrich) and Evan (Smotrycz), who love their Bears and Patriots – have become big Bills fans as well. Don't be surprised if you see them walking around campus in a Ryan Fitzpatrick jersey.

More importantly, we had our first full team workout over the weekend and it went really well. This was the first time since the day before the Duke game that the whole team was in the gym for practice and the coaches could watch.

We had about a 40-minute scrimmage with three teams of five and kept rotating teams in and out. After the scrimmage we had a little conditioning test that everyone loves doing so much. Three suicides in 30 seconds each with 30 seconds rest in between each one. Let me know if any of you can do that.

I thought the freshmen looked very good for their first real practice and while they have a lot to learn, it was a great start. The biggest jump you see is always in the sophomores and all of them have improved dramatically.

No matter how much you prepare for the season, there is nothing like college basketball. Just having that year of experience under your belt is so important. Colton (Christian) has improved his jump shot, Evan is a lot stronger and able to create for himself now, (Jon) Horford is a beast down low (even though he doesn't cut his nails and leaves cuts on everyone). Lastly, Timmy (Hardaway Jr.) has really worked on his ball handling and making reads of ball-screens because he will be used as a playmaker more this year.

I'm going to also start a new feature where I give you guys a drill we do and see if you can reach the goal the coaches' set for us.

The first drill is called 50-in-5 because you need to make 50 three's in five minutes. You get one ball and one rebounder and move around the arc trying to make 50 threes. The only rule is you cannot stand in one spot and get a rhythm. You must move around. The high on the team is 74 by Matt Vogrich, which is a ridiculous number. If you get 50 you win!

For a PDC (Player Development Center) update, apparently the plan is for everyone to move in on Oct. 10 with the first practice scheduled for the 14th. WE CANNOT WAIT!

While more and more information has been released as to what exactly will be in there, I can't tell you yet because it hasn't been released to the public. All I will say is that there is no way any other school in the country could have a facility like ours. I'm excited for you all to see it.

Lastly, in a fantasy update, I beat Zack (Novak), Jordan (Morgan) beat Stu (Douglass), Max (Bielfeldt) beat Blake (McLimans), Matt beat Jordan (Dumars) and Evan beat Sai (Tummala). I have the most points in the league and Dumars had the least.

Oh yea, if anyone can get 50-in-5 let me know and maybe we will bring you in for a workout.

I'll write again soon.

COUNTDOWN IS ON, NO MORE CONES, LOVE THE FANS & MAIZE RAGERS!

What's up everyone?

The countdown is on! There are only 16 days until we drop the ball and practice begins. It's crazy just how close it is, but the team is ready.

We have been continuing to do our routine of lifting, conditioning, open gyms and individuals, but if you ask anyone we are ready for Friday, October 14th. There are only so many cone drills, suicides and squats you can do before it is just time to play basketball. When practice begins is when the journey really starts. Each day you put in a little more, all preparing for our first goal – to win a Big Ten Championship.

Speaking of playing basketball, everyone got the chance to check out where we play and see just how good Crisler Arena looks. We had an open house last week and it was packed with people. I think everyone was in amazement with how much of a 180-degree transformation Crisler has taken.

We got to talk with all the fans and sign autographs for an hour. The most impressive thing about the event was how excited all the fans are for this season. The line for autographs was the longest I have ever seen and we probably could have stayed for another hour signing with the amount of people that were there. Everyone wanted to talk about how good they thought we were going to be and how many wins we should have. Most people said they have never been this excited for a basketball season.

Speaking of optimism, one of the most important things for this season is for us to remain hungry. You have to remember this is a new season and so far we haven't won a single game. It wasn't that long ago that no one thought we were going to be good and everyone picked against us.

Even though this year we might be the hunted and not the hunter, we must act like the hunter. If anything, our team must work even harder than last year. I have no doubt this is what the feeling in the locker room will be this year!

Last but definitely not least, I went to the Maize Rage opening meeting this week along with Zack (Novak) and Stu (Douglass). It is pretty cool to think that my freshman year they had 400 students and now it is at about 3,000.

I can't emphasize enough how much of a difference they make. We have the best student section in the Big Ten hands down. No one comes close. However, what I really learned this week is how much more they are than just a cheering section. Those guys do a ton of community service and travel all over helping people. Michigan is very lucky to have them! We are lucky to have them!

Finally, in a fantasy update, the standings after three weeks looks like this:

At a perfect 3-0 is Max Bielfeldt (somehow he got Sai (Tummala) to trade him Andre Johnson for garbage)

At 2-1: Evan Smotrycz (luckiest player so far) Jordan Morgan (I have no idea how his team has won a game, let alone two) Sai Tummala (His team is going down faster than the Red Sox)

At 1-2: Me (I am just shocked, but don't worry I won't be down here for long) Matt Vogrich (Too many Bears players, should never have let go of Olin Kruetz) Stu Douglass (Most disappointing team) Zack Novak (Team Green Bay doesn't look so good in fantasy) Blake McLimans (He is just so happy about the Bills he really isn't worrying about fantasy) Jordan Dumars (Still a solid member of the league, but Vick keeps getting hurt)

Have a great week!

Go Blue!

PRESEASON TESTS, THE JOKE, A BIG QUESTION AND A SHOUT OUT

What's up everyone?

It has been a little bit since I last blogged, but that is because we had our basketball "fall break" last weekend so I got to go home one last time. It was great to spend some time with the family! Hopefully the next time we get a weekend off will be right after we get back from New Orleans!

So getting started . . . let me say this first – a ton has happened in the last 10 days so let me catch you up.

First of all we had our preseason testing. This comprises of things like Mikan's, pulls up, long range buckets and other drills the coaches test us on to make sure we have been working on our games. In my three years here, this is by far the highest percent of guys who passed their tests on the first try – definitely a good sign.

We followed that with the gauntlet-conditioning test, which I can proudly say everyone passed on the first try as well. I have talked about the gauntlet before. Even the name sounds awful, it consists of two 17's (17 trips across the width of the floor in a minute) and an eight (eight trips across the width of the floor in a 30 seconds). If anyone out there can pass that I'd be extremely impressed.

The test that drew the most laughs however was the one we never actually did. This test would be a 20 rep, 185 pound squat test. I need to set up the joke first so that you will understand what happened.

We usually weight lift in two groups – eight people in the morning and eight people in the afternoon. One day, the morning group thought it would be funny, especially Zack (Novak) and Stu (Douglass), to have our strength coach, Adam Fletcher, text the afternoon group we were doing squat testing today. He knew everyone would be freaking out – especially Evan (Smotrycz) and Matt (Vogrich).

It worked 100 percent to perfection.

Matt was texting me all day gauging just how hard this would be and thinking about the consequences of not being able to accomplish it. My main man, Evan, did 20 reps of his body weight squats in his dorm room and admitted that it was really hard. Imagine a 6-10 basketball player in a little dorm room doing body weight squats all day – (HAHA).

They finally found out it was a joke when Coach Sanderson was pumping us up to get it done and just before we were going to start said, "Oh yea just do five reps, we aren't testing." You have never seen a happier group of people!

You must vote for a player because we all know Bacari (Alexander) is like the Beatles on Twitter. Please note that is an extremely serious matter so please vote on who you really think is the best. I can tell you everyone will be waiting on pins and needles for the results.

Now on to a more serious matter – practice officially starts tomorrow and we are more than ready. You can only accomplish so much during individual sessions, but once you get those 20 hour weeks, the journey really begins. Now that I have been here for a little bit, I can see how the coaches go about building on each day. We start with all the basics and each day build a little more. Everyone always wants to get to the games, but there is a process to getting there.

Key things we have to work on include transition defense, help side defense and of course our magical offense. But every college basketball team is starting at the same point right now. It is the teams that learn the quickest and build on each day that get off to great starts and sustain that all year long. That's our goal!

Last but not least, the fantasy football update section.

I have been taking a lot of heat for my team struggles, but it is just a health factor. My team is feeling good again and I fully expect to take off now. By far Jordan (Morgan) and Evan think their teams are the greatest things since sliced bread, so I almost feel as good about their teams losing as mine winning. Below are the standings.

FANTASY STANDINGS

Max, 4-1
Evan, 3-2
Zack, 3-2
Matt, 3-2
Jordan, 3-2
Stu, 3-2
Josh, 2-3
Sai, 2-3
Jordan Dumars, 2-3
Blake, 1-4

I will write again next week and have a ton to report on with how practice is going.

It's a great time to be a Michigan Wolverine with all the excitement going on in athletics. Good luck to football this weekend and Go Blue!

SHOUT OUT: Congrats to Alex Gatof who had the highest reported 50-in-5 of any of the fans with a shocking 63.

(NOTATION: A 50-in-5 is making a minimum of 50 three-pointers in five minutes.)

WEEK ONE DONE, THE KILLER B'S, BE THE VOICE, LEAVE THE LIGHTS ON!

What's up everyone?

The first week of Camp Wolverine is officially in the books. Six straight days of practice and I can say we are off to a great start. The past week was all about making sure we laid the groundwork and each day building off it.

When I talk about groundwork, I mean simple, but vital things like closeouts, defensive rotations and transition defense, just to name a few. If you notice all of those things have a commonality, which is defense. We can score as many points as we want, but if we don't shut people down on the defensive end, all that scoring means nothing. We drill defense everyday and it made a huge difference last year and I think you will see an even bigger one this year.

Our two freshman guards have really impressed me so far. Don't get me wrong they still have a ton to learn, (had to put that in there when they read this) but you can see why they came in so highly regarded. What I like best about both of them is how willing they are to learn. Coach B uses the analogy freshmen need to be like a sponge in soaking up all this knowledge they are receiving. I can tell you every opportunity possible Trey (Burke) and Carlton (Brundidge) have been asking a coach or a teammate a question whenever they need clarification.

On the court, Trey has really impressed me with his ability to pass the ball. He is seeing plays before they happen and making the simple pass. Carlton shoots the ball better than I realized. Everyone talks about his ability to slash and get to the rim, but he can also really shoot. "The Killer B's" will be making Michigan fans happy for a long time!

Off the court, Jordan (Morgan) is trying to get our whole team to watch Paranormal Activity 2 tonight. I, for one, can tell you there is no way I would ever go see a movie like that. I wouldn't be able to sleep for a week. Simply put – I just don't do scary movies. I almost went to see the first Paranormal Activity with Jordan two years ago and the next day all he and Corey (Person) talked about was how they had to leave the lights on when they went to sleep because they were so freaked out.

I don't forget those details.

It was a rough week fantasy wise for me again First, my quarterback gets hurt in the first quarter (thanks Jason Campbell) and then Peyton Hillis decided not to play the second half, so I lost to my arch nemesis Evan (Smotrycz). I wanted to win this week more than any other, but the fantasy gods just don't like me right now. I will rebound however.

Have a great week!

PUMPKIN CARVING, PARANORMAL ACTIVITY AND A SPECIAL GHOSTWRITER

BOO!

Hello blogosphere it is I, Evan "the great" Smotrycz.

I have been asked by Josh to do a special piece in light of Hallows Eve.

The other day I realized I have never carved a pumpkin, I vaguely remember watching my parents carve pumpkins when I was really young, but I have never done one myself. I am trying to organize a pumpkin carving with anyone that will join.

I am not big on being scared though, I can't watch scary movies. It seems as though everyone on the team outside of Josh and I could not wait to see the new Paranormal Activity movie. I am only a fan of comedy movies and would never pay to be scared, but to each his own.

I think that the biggest fan of the movie was by far J-Mo (Jordan Morgan). For a good week after the movie came out, that's all he would talk about. Due to his elongated rants on how scary the movie was, a few different debates on whether or not ghosts are real took place in the locker room. Eso (Akunne) ran the point in these discussions offering many different possibilities of thought.

On another note, practice has been going well. Everyone has been working hard and taking personal accountability in order to get ready for the season. We seem to be in good shape and shooting the ball very well.

This is probably the most exciting part of the season for me – for the most part preseason is over and games are about to start. It will be nice to play against people who aren't on our team. All summer we have been playing pickup games against each other and we finally get to play other teams. It will be nice to get a look at the new Player Development Center. I know our coaches have already moved in and say it's amazing, but I have yet to catch even the slightest glimpse of anything.

The suspense is killing me, but I have no doubt that it will be worth the wait.

I know that my blogging skills are way behind Josh's so please do not compare me to a seasoned veteran. I know Josh gets rave reviews, so much so that whenever a new Bartelstein blog is released my mom calls me and proceeds to tell me how he should be in journalism.

Seeing as I am now in somewhat of a position of power now I have to take advantage. I would like to take this opportunity to let everyone know that I have the best fantasy team and am not worried about any of the competition.

I have Tom Brady leading the way and (knock on wood) do not expect him to lose again anytime soon, especially to a team like the Bills. Josh's team stinks and he continues to blame it on injury problems, yet he continues to call himself a "fantasy guru." I will stop at that at the risk of abusing my power.

We have a great group of guys who are hungry for wins and blessed to be playing in the Maize and Blue. I can't wait to see and hear our fans at our first real game in the new Crisler Arena. In the words of Bacari Alexander "Grow Blue" and follow me on twitter @_ev23. I am out!

IPADS, POETS, THE FIRST GAME AND A BIG THANK YOU

What's up everyone? I'm back.

As I'm sure most of you have heard already, we have officially moved into the PDC (Player Development Center). There are pictures and videos all over the Michigan Facebook page and MGoBlue.com that you need to check out. I'm sure in the coming days more will be put up.

I have seen a lot of facilities over the years from college all the way to the pros and I can honestly say nothing is as nice as our facility. Everything is top notch from the offices to the film room (more like a movie theatre) to the locker room (we each have our own iPad) to the hot and cold tubs in the training room. Everything is perfect.

The iPad's are going to be used for a ton of different things. For one, they are our locker name plates but more importantly they will be used for scouting reports and breaking down video. Instead of printing out hundreds of pages of paper, everything will be on our iPad.

We can watch clips of practice or games and break down player tendencies. For some people like Eso (Akunne) and Corey (Person) the most important function will be blasting their rap music. You can hear them a mile away because they will be laughing and singing some rap song I personally can't even understand.

Expanding on that, Michigan basketball is very diverse. Not only are we into music, but we also chant poetry. No I'm not kidding, we have a tradition the night before each game that we call our position coach and say a poem that proves we are ready for the game.

We had a trial session this weekend before a big practice and Sai (Tummala) took it to a whole new level. Most of the time people will say a simple poem like "Roses are Red, Violets are Blue, I'm ready for tomorrow and I know you are too."

Well Sai being the great poet he is, researched a Robert Frost poem, and chanted it off to Coach Meyer, something I can guarantee in all Coach Beilein's years has never be done. I think it is safe to say we have a young Ernest Hemingway on our team.

Now back to the actual game of basketball.

We are really excited to play our first exhibition game on Friday (Nov. 4) against Wayne State. We want to show off all the hard work that has been put in the last three weeks and play against someone other than ourselves.

I'm also excited to see all the fans that are in for a big surprise with their first look at Crisler. I have a feeling Crisler is going to be rocking on Friday night! We know there is hockey that night as well, but we cannot wait to see you all there.

The fantasy standings are staying away from the blog this week for personal reasons, but they will be back in better times.

Also, I plan on giving away some tickets to home games this year so to see how you can win tickets to our games stay tuned!!

Next time out, I will break down the game against Wayne State! Until then, Go Blue!

AN IMPORTANT P.S. – My teammates and I need to thank everyone who had a part in making this facility possible. We were talking last night how much we take for granted some times, however, we really appreciate all the work that went into the PDC and promise to show our gratitude on the court. So to the university, Dave Brandon, the entire athletic department, donors, all our coaches, the workers, architects and anyone else who helped make this possible, a huge THANK YOU!

11/11/2011

ONE GAME AT A TIME, THE COLD TUB KING, FANTASY SORROWS

What's up everyone?

The season has officially arrived. Our first game that counts on our record is tonight (Friday, Nov. 11) against Ferris State. We cannot wait to get out on the court in front of our fans and tip off the new season. It is a very exciting time because every team has goals ahead of them they think they can achieve and we are no different. We have big goals we plan to accomplish this year, but it all happens one game at a time.

Before anything else, I have give a big shout out to our fans who showed up in big numbers first the exhibition game. It was by far the most fans we have had since I've been here for an exhibition and you guys were really loud. I always tell people we have the loudest home court advantage in the Big Ten and you proved me right again. I can't wait to see how loud it is going to be tonight.

Since our exhibition game last Friday (Nov. 4), we have had in my opinion are best week of practice this year. We went really hard, cleaning up some things from the game but also just working on keys to us having success this year. Coach Beilein always says the biggest jump in your learning curve comes after that first exhibition game and I think he is 100 percent right.

A funny thing has happened now that we are officially moved into the PDC.

Corey Person has joined the movement of getting in the cold tub after practice. For the first two years I have been here, the coaches after practice have always said get in the cold tubs and almost never would Corey get in them. The tubs were not "cool" by any means. Now that we have these huge cold and hot tubs, Corey pretty much lives in them. The only person who spends more time in them is Evan (Smotrycz), but he is almost an exclusive hot tub guy. You would think he was on vacation in the Caribbean sometimes.

From a fantasy standpoint, these first eight weeks have been very hard on me. I've lost hours of sleep and it has been hard to focus in class – no not really.

I thought I drafted not a good but a great team. My issues are as follows: First Peyton Hillis decided he didn't want to play this year and every time he practices he re-inures his hamstring. Miles Austin has not only pulled his left hamstring but then later pulled his right. Hakeem Nicks pulled his hamstring. Do you see a pattern yet? Not to mention Philip Rivers is playing like he has no hamstrings. So these are my excuses for my struggles.

Below are the standings:

Max: 8-1 Evan: 6-3 Zack: 5-4 Matt: 5-4 J-Mo: 5-4 Stu: 4-5 Sai: 4-5 Blake: 3-6 Josh: 3-6 Dmnars: 2-7

On a very important note, I will be giving four tickets away to our game this Thursday (Nov. 17) against Western Illioois.

THE BIG 10 DAY TRIP, THE BIG WIN, THE BIG MONDAY SURPRISE

What's up everyone?

Not a bad time to be a University of Michigan fan. First the football team plays Nebraska on Saturday – don't forget it is Military Appreciation Day. We hear there are big things planned for the game. Too bad we are going to miss it because after playing Western Illinois tonight, we head on to the most prestigious Thanksgiving tournament in the country – the Maui Invitational. I have a feeling there is going to be a lot of Maize and Blue being worn around the next week or so.

Backtracking just a bit, we had a good win Monday night against Towson. One thing that sticks out is how well we are playing defensively. I'm not surprised because in practice we have really been focusing on our key concepts in what we what to accomplish every possession down the court.

The key to our defense is keeping people out of the "club," which is the paint, and we are the bouncers at the door who aren't supposed to let anyone in. You can thank the one and only Bacari Alexander for this analogy. Over the past two years Michigan basketball has put a whole new emphasis on what defense means. Our goal is to win a national championship and you only do that by playing great defense.

After beating Towson on Monday night, we had Tuesday off to take care of school work and rest up for what is going to be a crazy 10 days. Let me break down our schedule for everyone.

We will play a game in Ann Arbor, fly to Hawaii, play three games against some of the top teams in the country, fly back on Thanksgiving, rest, practice, leave for Charlottesville on Monday and play our ACC/Big Ten Challenge in Virginia on Tuesday. That is a ton of traveling. Feel free to calculate the total miles. So it is going to be an interesting time for us. We just ask you stay with us and cheer us on! We cannot wait to get back to Crisler on Dec. 3 against Iowa State – yea, another big game!!

On a side note, I will be curious to see the diehard Green Bay fan Zack Novak try to figure out how to watch the Lions-Packers game while we are flying back. Stay tuned for that story.

More important than any basketball game or future game was my huge fantasy win over Jordan Morgan this past Sunday. For the past two months, I've taken a ton of verbal abuse from everyone on our team, especially J-Mo.

So when I beat him this week, actually more like crushed him, I really couldn't have felt any better about it. I tweeted about it, Facebooked it and now I'm blogging about it so everyone knows that I beat him. Just want to make that crystal clear.

Now on to some important notes about Maui.

I will try and provide as many updates as I can while we are there. Everything about what we are doing during our free time to game information. I also have to tell everyone that we have a surprise for you in what we will be wearing Monday afternoon I can't give out any more information than that, but it will blow some of you away!

Go Blue!

11/21/2011

ALOHA, SNORKELS, BLACK CRAB, CAN'T THROW ANYMORE AND NBA JAMS

Aloha everyone!

All I can say is after spending two days here it is going to be hard going back to Ann Arbor. The weather is perfect and just being in the sun puts you in a good mood! Now I want to provide you all with a quick update before I run off the film.

So far the trip has been a lot of fun.

We have had two very spirited practices that have focused on preparing for Memphis, but also fixing some things that we need to do better. At this point I think we are all ready to play Memphis and get this tournament going.

Besides basketball, we have had some time to explore all Hawaii has to offer. A bunch of us went snorkeling today and saw some fish and even a black crab. Tim was extremely excited to see the crab.

They also have a cliff that you can jump off of and everyone on our team was scared to try it, (probably the right move) but Evan's sister stepped right up and showed us all how it's done.

We played some water football in the pool where I found out my arm has become awful. I'm not saying it was very good in the first place, but now my ball is flying all over kind like Tim Tebow. It is actually very disheartening.

Another very important part of our trip that didn't involve basketball was the EA Sports video game challenge. That took place last night with every team sending two players up to play NBA Jam. We were represented by Evan (Smotrycz) and Tim (Hardaway Jr.), both who claimed to be excellent at NBA Jam.

Of course we played Memphis in the first round, and it was a thrilling game. After getting off to a very slow start, Evan and Tim kicked into high gear with Evan draining three after three. We had a seven point lead with about a minute left, but some bad turnovers and a clutch three led to a tough defeat. We will be more than ready to play them Monday when the game actually counts.

With that I'm off to watch some film and talk about our keys to beating Memphis tomorrow.

Make sure you guys all tune in tomorrow at 3pm on ESPN. I'll try to write again tomorrow night!

Go Blue!

CAN'T SLEEP, DREAM GAMES, THE KEYS TO MEMPHIS WIN, EMAIL BAG

Aloha everyone!

It's 6:30 in the morning and I've had enough sleep.

I'd bet most of the team is up right now just waiting to get on that bus and head on over to play Duke. These are the types of games we all dream of playing, the reason we chose the University of Michigan: to play in headline games on ESPN.

Yesterday was a great day. I can't tell you how impressed I was with Trey (Burke). He really showed everyone he is as tough as they come and competed with another really good point guard for all 40 minutes. Trey is going to be a key for us all year and I have a feeling his confidence is going to just keep getting higher and higher.

Another two guys who deserve a ton of credit are Evan (Smotrycz) and Matt (Vogrich). Everyone knows they can really shoot, but what stuck out yesterday was their ability to impact the game even when their three ball isn't going in.

Matt was huge in taking charges and really changing the game because Memphis didn't want to go in the lane anymore. Evan was gigantic on the glass and you guys should all be able to notice how much of a difference that extra weight has made. This is a huge step for both of them.

Time to move on from Memphis, now we have another very difficult test today. We already started preparing for Duke last night and it will continue this morning. There is only so much you can do in 24 hours, but our coaches will do it all. No one is better in preparation in the country.

I know everyone is talking about last year's NCAA game. It's a new year, a new team and a new focus. Do we think about it, yes. However we need to make sure we stick to what we want to do this season.

Lastly, even though we are in Maui, fantasy football still is a topic of discussion. My team had a huge win over Zack (Novak) and now I'm just a game out of the playoff picture. All year I said just wait for my team to get healthy and now we are making our run.

Maybe the best comments will receive tickets to an upcoming game again!

THE WINS, THE FLIP, MY JUMP AND ONTO THE CHALLENGE

What's up everyone?

What a great weekend to be part of the Michigan family and a Michigan fan. First and foremost, I have to give out huge congratulations to the football team on its big win against Ohio! I know how hard they worked all year to beat them and it was great to see it on Saturday. The scene after the game is what makes Michigan special because no one else in the country can replicate.

On the basketball front, we had a nice win over UCLA on Wednesday. They are a talented team that before the end of the year will have a bunch of wins in the Pac-12. We needed to bounce back after that tough loss to Duke and I think that's what was most impressive about the win.

As a team, we really follow our two senior leaders in Zack (Novak) and Stu (Douglass). They both had big games against UCLA and that should be expected. Some teams would have a tough time getting up for that game, but when your leaders are bringing energy and knocking down shots like they did, it is infectious to the whole team. Also, I never thought I'd see the day Zack would actually break the 20point barrier. He was stuck at 20, but finally broke through with that 22-point performance. Finally!

After we beat UCLA, we had the afternoon off to enjoy Maui. This was very good for a couple of reasons. One, Stu was going to be the only person ever to go to Maui and never see the sun. He never came outside until after the UCLA game and if not for that last afternoon, he would have left Maui whiter than he came.

Our hotel had this huge cliff that all week people talked about jumping off of. We just needed to wait until after the completion of our games. The most impressive thing about the cliff jumping was my new road roommate, Carlton Brundidge, doing a flip off the cliff.

Yes, I said FLIP.

It was extremely impressive, but shouldn't be surprising because CB was on the swimming team in high school and no I am not joking. It allowed me to prove to everyone that I could and would jump off that cliff. The only thing we never found out was if Corey Person could swim. He had a bet with Jordan (Morgan) all week, but mysteriously got sick that afternoon. We are still investigating the incident.

Now that most of us are recovered from going to Maui – it took a while to get used to the time change – we get to leave Ann Arbor again today to head to Virginia. This will be a very difficult game against a good ACC team, but a win we need to get – you remember how important the win at Clemson was last year.

With that, I'm off the practice and then to the airport.

Don't forget, I will be giving away four more tickets to Saturday's game against Iowa State.

12/8/2011
RESILIENCY, THREE THINGS ABOUT MAX AND THE FANTASY STRETCH RUN

What's up everyone?

A lot has happened since I last wrote, especially because our schedule has been crazy. This is by far the most games we have played before finals since I have been here and clearly the most traveling we have done.

Saturday was a good test for us. Iowa State is an extremely talented team that has a bunch of former Big Ten players on it. But more importantly, we needed to show resiliency and bounce back. After a real tough loss at Virginia, losing two in a row was not an option, especially a game at home.

We took care of business, which is what you have to do when you play in the best conference in America. It is hard enough to win games in the Big Ten, however, the best teams are the ones that can rebound from tough losses and take care of their home court. That needs to be part of our identity all year, so it was great to see it Saturday.

I have received a bunch of questions on Max Bielfeldt.

Things you need to know about Max: One, he has the biggest calves in the world. Two, he sets a mean screen and by the time he graduates, it may be up there with Graham Brown. Three, he is the next Brian Cardinal – can really shoot, strong as heck and plays the game the right way.

Okay, on a serious note, Max is doing great and continues to get better and better. It is amazing how much freshmen improve in just a short time. Once he got comfortable with our routine every day, he has started to play really well. His time will come and until then he is an extremely important member of the scout team.

All year long, I have written in this blog just to be patient with my fantasy team. Everyone had given up on my squad, but I kept hope and knew when my team got healthy, good things would happen. Sure enough with one week to go in the season, I have moved into fourth place and a win this week means I make the playoffs. (I don't see Jordan Morgan making the playoffs, do you?)

Here are the updated standings: Max 12-1 Evan 9-4 Stu 7-6 Josh 7-6 Zack 7-7 Matt 6-7 Jordan 6-7 Blake 5-8 Sai 5-8 JD 2-11 I hope we see a ton of Michigan fans at the Palace this Saturday against Oakland. They are a very talented team who has already knocked off Tennessee for the second time in two years.

THE RECAPS, THE RETURN OF RORY, THE SCARF AND THE PLAYOFFS

What's up everyone?

I'm taking a break from studying from finals so I can give you an update on the team. We have had two more games since I last wrote, an offensive masterpiece against Oakland and a sloppy win over Arkansas-Pine Bluff – which we have to give them a ton of credit for competing to the end.

The Oakland game was a lot of fun for a couple reasons. One, playing at the Palace of Auburn Hills was a very cool experience and it was great to see so many Michigan fans out there, just proving again why you are the best.

Also, my man Rory, who I wrote about a ton last year, was at the game and I got to talk to him for a little. He is doing great; his cancer is in remission and he is back in school and cheering on Michigan as loud as ever. There is no doubt the reason we made 15 threes and scored 90 points was because he was there. It also helps when Timmy (Hardaway Jr.), Trey (Burke) and Stu (Douglass) are on fire.

The day after the Oakland game, I got to the gym early to get some extra shots up and Corey (Person) was already in there shooting. When I was looking at his shot, something didn't seem right and after a few minutes Matt (Vogrich) and myself figured out exactly what it was – Corey was shooting with a women's ball!

Now two things quickly came to my mind – one, why was he making so many shots and two, I cannot make fun of Illinois and Oakland anymore for playing with a women's ball for the first half of their game last year because now one of our own had fallen into the same trap. Matt and I watched from the corner for a while and then just asked him if he noticed anything a little different with his ball. Of course, he had no clue until we threw him a men's ball and immediately the shot didn't look the same.

Okay, changing it up a bit. I was very proud of Tim this week and it had nothing to do with basketball. Ever since Tim arrived on campus last year, he has tried to dress like me and partially like Evan (Smotrycz). I have tried to teach him the tricks of the trade, but it has been a slow process. Well, this week Tim showed up to practice with a scarf on. Yes, a scarf! I knew the transformation was complete.

Tim would never have worn a scarf before coming here. Now I know he came from Miami, which means he would have no use for the scarf, but it was the sophistication of the look that proved to me a light bulb had gone off. For me personally, I'm not a scarf guy; however, Evan is, so he deserves some credit for that. It is great to know Tim has hatched from his cocoon and doesn't need me anymore. My little Timmy has grown so much! HA!

Onto more important matters – fantasy football playoffs started this week.

The matchups are Max (Bielfeldt) against me in the 1-4 game and Evan against Stu in 2-3. As a said all along, my team would make the playoffs and sure enough I don't see all my haters like Matt, Zack (Novak) and Jordan (Morgan) listed above.

I will update you onsemifinals next week

We hope to see you at Crisler for our next two games against Alabama A&M and Bradley (return of Patrick Beilein). Your support is always needed and appreciated.

GREAT THREE DAYS, RETURN OF THE DOBO AND EVAN WON?

What's up everyone?

I hope you all had a great holiday and I, and the team, want to wish you a very Happy New Year coming up this Satruday. Another new year!

We just got back from a nice three-day break where almost everyone went home to see their family. For Colton (Christian) that is going all the way to Seattle, Wash., and for Eso (Akunne) just around the corner off Main Street. No matter what the distance was, it is great for everyone to be able to see their family and sleep in their bed for a couple nights. Plus, there is nothing like a home cooked meal from your mom.

Everyone returned to campus Monday night and we are back in the swing of things getting ready for our Big Ten opener against Penn State tonight. Before I can talk about Penn State, I want to go back to the Bradley game.

For one, the fans were outstanding! You guys were so loud and created an atmosphere that is unmatched in the Big Ten. The other reason was because it marked the return of Pat Beilein to Ann Arbor.

Pat is Coach Beilein's son who worked as a grad assistant for Michigan my freshman year and is now the director of basketball operations at Bradley. For me, Pat was a huge help both on and off the court. He is someone who I really looked up to and still do (hopefully he doesn't read this) and will always be a friend.

Pat was a member of the scout team and he could really fill it up as long as we played in the half court. Once we started to run a little, he was always trailing the play. He would want to me let you all know (he reminded me a lot) that he did in fact score 1,000 points at West Virginia as crazy as it sounds, so him making shots in scout team shouldn't come as a surprise. I have no doubt Pat will be a head coach one day because of great he is with the X's and O's of the game, but as good as he is with that, he is an even better guy!

Now, onto a much more somber matter, somehow Evan (Smotrycz) won the fantasy football league. I really have no idea how this happened because this is the guy who drafted nine wide receivers, including Brian Hartline. I have to give him credit because he pulled it off.

I have lost and will continue to lose sleep over this matter as he knocked me out in the semifinals, but I promise next year he will not finish ahead of me. Max (Bielfeldt) came in second and Stu (Douglass) came in fourth.

Next time I write hopefully we have two great Big Ten wins at home and Crisler will have been packed to the top. If not to watch some great basketball, you have got to come and check out the alunmi band as they get the place rocking.

Be safe and have a great New Year!

1/9/2012

THE BIG GAMES, THE LEGENDS, THE WII, THE SMOOTHIE KING

What's up everyone?

I want to wish everyone a very Happy New Year and one that hopes to have many special moments for our basketball team!

It was big week for us last week as we had to face back-to-back ranked teams.

It was a very tough loss at Indiana. First off, Indiana is a very good team and losing to them at Assembly Hall is nothing to be embarrassed about, especially by just two points and being down by as much as 15. However, for the goals we want to accomplish, that is a game we expect to win. We had our chances down the stretch. As Coach Beilein pointed out the next day, there were a ton of mistakes we made during the first 38 minutes of the game that cost us the win. We believe that, although some of these mistakes are small, once we clean it up our team is going to make a huge jump and really be special to watch.

So how did we respond?

We had a great win against Wisconsin. It was truly a special day to be a Wolverine. We got to talk and meet three Michigan greats – Cazzie Russell, Rudy Tomjanovich and Phil Hubbard – before the game. I mean, three of the five jerseys hanging from the rafters were in the locker room. If we weren't pumped up before that, I am not sure what to tell you.

I can tell you everyone was ready to go after Cazzie spoke. He spoke about how much he loves watching our team play because we play tough and, most importantly, together. What will stick with me the most, however, is that Cazzie said watching us play makes him proud to be a Michigan Man and we all represent everyone that comes before us. Very, very powerful stuff.

Onto the game. I was really impressed with our team defense. Wisconsin offers a ton of challenges when you play them. The first being you must guard them for the full 35-second shot clock, or as we said 36 seconds.

The next thing to talk about is how everyone has been so impressed with Trey (Burke) on offense this year, but Trey proved again why he is having such a great year on defense. Wisconsin's Jordan Taylor had to work very hard for all his shots. Trey just did a terrific job along with Stu (Douglass), but by this point we all expect this from Stu.

I need to give a big shoutout to Jordan (Morgan), who is playing with a swagger again and attacking the boards. When J-Mo plays like this, our team is really hard to play against because we get extra possessions. J-Mo's hunger and effort the last couple of games has just been outstanding.

Overall, it was just a great win for us and snapping that losing streak wasn't too shabby either.

Shifting gears just a tad.

The other very important game of the week did not take place on the court but rather in a video game. Our new locker room has a Wii system that the team spends countless hours playing. The game of choice is Super Smash Brothers – pretty much choose a character and try to destroy each other – and after dinner the other day I did some investigating at who is

REALLY the best (note: I say really because at some point each guy on our team has self-appointed himself as the best).

The first thing I found out is that Eso (Akunne) is the Cazzie Russell of Smash, while Corey (Person) definitely is not. Apparently, he picked up his first win the other day (only took three months). The cheapest player is – of course – Evan (Smotrycz) because he spends the entire game hiding until the end and tries to swindle his way to a win. The player most out of touch with reality – meaning he thinks he is way better than he is – would be Jon (Horford). Lastly, (Zack) Novak has not played a game yet, because he is training at home until he believes he will dominate everyone in the locker room. Something only he would do.

Another competition our team has been having lately is who can make the best milkshake. With all of our team meals, we are always able to create our own milkshakes/smoothies for dessert.

In the past, Jon was pretty much known as the "Smoothie King," to the point that he could work at a Dairy Queen. But Jordan (Morgan), who got his own apartment this year (meaning now he has his own blender to practice with) may have become the new leader.

I am a definitely a believer in J-Mo and he now supplies me with my smoothies daily. So the good news for Jordan is: if this whole basketball thing doesn't work out, he is talented enough to work for DQ!

Lastly, be on the lookout for The Journey this Sunday (Jan. 14). It is one of my favorite shows on TV and they do a terrific job of capturing what the Big Ten is all about. This week they will have a feature on Novak and the crew came to our house today to check out our pad. We cleaned up very nicely for it, but there are definitely some funny moments that will air Sunday night! I cannot wait to see how it turns out.

With that I'm off to sleep as we play Northwestern on Wednesday (Jan. 11) and need to keep momentum going on what will hopefully be a long winning streak.

THE GAME, THE FUN, THE DEFENDER, THE ROOKIE

WHAT IS UP EVERYONE!

What a game! What a night! This is why being a part of Michigan basketball is so special.

Games like that make all the running, all the lifting, all the drills and all the practices worth it!

People always ask what this rivalry means to us. There is no doubt we want to beat Michigan State and there is a dislike between the two teams. However, Coach Beilein said it best when he said our fans really care a great deal about this game, which makes me care a lot also.

There is nothing better than seeing Crisler rocking and everyone going nuts. That is what we are all about. As a program we define FUN as doing something well together. Last night I think a whole lot of people had FUN.

I really hope all of our fans appreciate what Stu (Douglass) does for this team. Yes, he is a great shooter and makes smart choices on offense, but you need to watch Stu play defense. He works his tail off every game many times guarding the best guard on the other team. I think he might be the best in the country at getting through screens. It is exhausting just watching him. We would be nowhere close to where we are today without Stu.

The other big question of the night was would Trey (Burke) understand what this game means? Does anyone still wonder?

I never had a doubt Trey would play a great game because that is just what he does. Whether it is open gym or playing in a game like last night, Trey is a big time player. He loves the moment and that three he hit from way deep was the biggest shot of the night. The best part with him is how humble he is and he just acts like this is what he is supposed to do. It is great being Trey's teammate, he just gets it.

One of the cool parts in playing in games like last night is that the media coverage is immense. One of the best writers out there, Jeff Goodman from CBSSports.com (check out his article on Trey), was at the game and he has a tradition of putting the MVP of the day as his avatar on twitter.

Well today his avatar is a combination of Zack (Novak) and Trey, so make sure you check him out because he writes great stuff, plus his nephew (Josh Mack) is one of our team managers, so he has that Michigan connection, even though he went to Arizona.

Lastly, make sure you tune into The Journey on Sunday because you need to see what the locker room was like last night. There is nothing I can say that will describe the emotions of it, but let's just say we had a lot of FUN!

We have a tough run ahead of us with five of the next six games on the road, but I know you will be there right along side us!

Go Blue!

1/23/2012

RESOLVE & TOUGHNESS, OUR MOXIE, NO EASY SCHEDULE

What's up everyone?

I just got back from practice after a tough loss yesterday. A lot of people would think the atmosphere today would be somber, but it couldn't have been any different. We were all upbeat and just excited to get back on the court and get better.

No question we expect to win every game and there are no moral victories when you are trying to win a championship, but the resolve and toughness we showed yesterday is the reason I think this group can really accomplish some special stuff this year.

Winning on the road is really hard, if you didn't already know that from watching college basketball this year. We had about 19,000 fans screaming at us as soon as we got off the bus, and it was Arkansas' first sellout in almost three years. Between that and Arkansas getting a chance to play Michigan on national television, we knew we were going to get their best show. We would not want it any other way.

Coach Beilein tells us all the time when you go on the road, you better expect to get a team's A game. The reason he says this is because of the name across our jerseys. Everyone gets up to play when they play against Michigan; that's the reason every road game we play is sold out.

Now, onto the game.

Arkansas came out on fire, making their first 11 shots and it took us a while to get used to their speed. I have to say Arkansas is really, really quick. But after the first eight minutes of the game, we really settled in and dominated the game.

The problem was we dug ourselves a huge hole and just couldn't get over the top. I think our performance was really an indicator of the moxie of our team and just how tough we have become. A lot of teams would have folded once they found themselves down 20 on the road, but not this team.

That's the biggest difference in my time at Michigan. We have become a team that hits the ground first, takes charges and does all the ugly stuff that winners do. We have become both mentally and physically tough!

Our schedule doesn't get any easier as today we leave to take on Purdue on Tuesday (Jan. 24). They are another very talented team who really gets after you on defense just like Arkansas. We will be ready to go and try to remain in first place in the Big Ten. Make sure you all tune in Tuesday night on ESPN!

Before I go, I want to just say I appreciate all the comments I get on how much fun our team is to watch. We know we have great fans and we try to represent Michigan the way it should be. That means playing as hard as anyone and having a ton of energy and enthusiasm for the game every time out.

I have also had a ton of questions about Stu Douglass' defense. Stu is a big time defender and, yes, as many of you have pointed out, re rever gets the credit he deserves. Next time we play, check out how hard he works on defense every possession One of the best in the country! Go Blue!

2/1/2012

THE OHIO GAME, THE FUNNY STORY, THE VOTES FOR COACH

What's up everyone?

We are coming off a tough loss against Ohio, one in which we didn't feel like we played our best, but we have to give them credit for playing pretty good on their home court. However, the best part of that game is they have to make the trip to Ann Arbor and play in front of our great fans. We will be more than ready for the return matchup. Remember that game we will also have College GameDay on campus! It should be a great atmosphere at Crisler.

Before we can even think about Ohio, we must focus on Indiana, who we play tonight.

We lost to them in Bloomington, Ind., in what was a very good game. However, it was a game where we made mistakes that we shouldn't make and have improved upon since then. When we watched the tape of the game in practice yesterday, we saw how much better we are in so many areas since that first time we met. We know Indiana is great in transition and plays at an extremely fast pace. It will be a key for us winning tomorrow and something we have worked on the last couple days of practice.

Now it may be hard for us to simulate the speed of Indiana, but we have a secret weapon that no other team in the country has. That secret weapon is the one and only LaVall Jordan.

For the last couple of weeks, Coach Jordan has continued to help out our scout team by being that speed demon he "thinks" he is on the court. In all seriousness, coach Jordan is a really good player; he starred at Butler, played overseas and in the D league.

I have talked about it before, but for a young point guard, there is no one better to learn from than coach Jordan. On the court however, he at times can over dribble. I can remember a couple too many times I have been wide open and coach Jordan has taken a questionable shot instead. We might have to break down the film of him coming up if this continues.

Now onto one of the funnier stories that has taken place at my time in Michigan.

Actually, it is second only to the Corey Pearson falling on top of a ball story that I think I have shared with everyone. It involves Matt Sawyer, one of our head managers – who does a great job, but I have to tell this story.

Matt and all the managers work very hard at rebounding basketballs during practice, but especially before a game. Everyone is on edge and it is important guys get their shots up. Well a couple games ago, Matt was rebounding under the basket and he was about to throw a ball out to Zack Novak when at the same time Sai Tummala threw a ball from under the basket. (Important side note: don't mess with captain Zack before a game).

In what seemed like slow motion, the balls collided and one ball hit Matt in a place a guy never wants to ever be hit. He was in an incredible amount of pain, rolling on the court for what seemed like minutes.

What made this even more interesting was that fact that warm-ups were over and the national anthem was about to begin.

It was a race against the clock, what would happen first, Matt getting off the ground or the start of the national anthem? I was about to send our trainer John (DoRosario) over to check him out, but Matt just made it to the bench in time. He reported no lingering effects from the traumatic event!

One last very important note, Coach Beilein is competing in an event to raise money for a charity of his choosing. Coach B is all about giving back and now it is time for all our great Michigan fans to vote for coaches Charity.

Click on this link, it takes two seconds and it will do a lot of good for a lot of people. Plus, anything that puts coach in a good mood is great.

With that I'm off to class, but I cannot wait to see our great crowd at Crisler tonight – should be a big-time game!

Go Blue!

TEAM EFFORT, CELINE, UPDATE OF A FEW FORMER WOLVERINES

What's up everyone?

Hope you guys are a lot more energized than I am right now. I didn't get back to my house until 3 a.m., however after a win it doesn't really matter. Coach Beilein always says his favorite wins over the years have come on the road because it takes a total team effort.

This was the case last night at Nebraska and everyone on our team played a big role – from Zack (Novak) and Stu (Douglass) dropping threes, to Tim (Hardaway Jr.) attacking the basket in the second half and Matt (Vogrich) catching fire in the second half. Matt did what we see him do every day in practice, so it was great to see those shots fall during a game.

There is a reason Matt caught fire last night. First, coach Alexander (BA) realized that Matt and Blake (McLimans) are always sitting next to each other. They are connected at the hip – they live together, room together on the road, sit across from each other on the plane and eat every meal next to each other. It is safe to say wherever you see one, the other will be right behind.

Once BA pointed this out, Matt and Blake purposely didn't sit next to each other during our team meal before the game. So this could be one key. The other being that Matt and Blake were listening to Celine Dion in their room the night before the game. Coach Jordan was doing room checks and he walked in and Matt and Blake were rocking to Celine. So I think whoever is in charge of music at Crisler needs to put some Celine on before the game and Matt will guarantee at least three trey balls!

That game closed a stretch where we played five out of six games on the road and something I hope we don't ever have to do again. I know my first two years here we definitely never had anything like that, but it is an exhausting stretch.

The last week was the most tired I have been in a long time and it stems from all the travel, not sleeping in your own bed and arriving in the wee hours of the morning. One thing it does is make you appreciate playing at home. That's why we cannot wait to get back on the court Sunday at Crisler and not leave again for 10 days!

I've received a few questions about if I ever talk to guys who we have played with but left or graduated over the past few years.

First of all, I promised DeShawn Sims I would give him a shoutout, but yes I talk to a ton of the guys who I've played with. DeShawn is playing professionally overseas and killing it over there. He made the all-star team and even competed in the dunk contest. Not sure how that happened because DeShawn wasn't exactly the best dunker I've seen.

Manny Harris is playing in the D-League and really playing well. He is averaging almost 20 points a game and I think he will be called up to the NBA very soon.

Lastly, Darius Morris is on the Lakers and will be on the team the rest of the year as his contract was guaranteed. He tells me he is learning from Kobe every day, not a bad person to learn from and I think D-Mo will have a great career ahead of him. He is one of the hardest workers I have ever been around.

Hopefully I see a ton of you Sunday when we take on the Illini. They are a good team and we need a great crowd to start a winning streak and keep our home record perfect!

2/15/2012

A LITTLE WIN STREAK, NOT JUST SCORING, GAMEDAY!

What's up everyone?

Not a bad week for us, playing two games and getting two wins? We needed to get on a little win streak here and sure enough we did. We now stand at 19-7 and 9-4 in the Big Ten, just a half game out of first place.

This is a very unique blog in that as we speak, I am being filmed by TV cameras and being asked questions about what this blog means to all Michigan fans and me. They are doing a segment for Coach Beilein's TV show – Inside Michigan Basketball – airing Monday nights at 7 p.m. on FSN-Detroit.

So, I have to say this is a pretty cool experience. Definitely the most pressure I have ever had in writing a blog. I have a time limit to get this all done!

The next three weeks are sure to be a wild ride and it all starts Saturday when we take on Ohio State with College GameDay coming into town. However, before I can get into that, I must first talk about Tim Hardaway Jr. and all he is doing for our team – some of which you don't see in a boxscore.

As we have all heard, Tim has been in a little bit of a shooting slump over the last month – last year

he never missed, so the expectations continue to be high. However, I think for our team and especially for Tim, this is going to be a blessing in disguise.

For one, Tim has learned to contribute in so many more aspects than last year. His rebounding has improved a ton, he is making plays at the basket, he is sharing the ball, and defensively compared to last year he is a different player. For those who really watch the game – watch Tim off the ball on defense and look at how he's seeing where the ball is a ton better. When Tim does all of this, it makes our team that much more dangerous! Sometimes it is not just about stats. There is no one who wants to help us win more than Tim. You need to know he is doing just that, helping us win.

Okay, now onto one of the more exciting things that is going to take place this weekend.

ESPN's College GameDay will be spending the day at Crisler Center on Saturday. I think Coach Beilein said it best, it is pretty much going to be a daylong commercial for Michigan basketball. We are very excited for all the hoopla and activities that comes with something like this, but more importantly, we need to maintain focus on the game.

I know the Maize Rage will be ready as I attended their meeting this week and they were bouncing ideas off me for about 30 minutes. They are going to be at Crisler about four hours early camping out and getting mentally ready to get inside Ohio State's heads. There is a reason they are an elite student section and this weekend is an opportunity for them to show off their skills, along with all the rest of our fans.

The key to the whole day is trying to make it seem like just a typical game, not getting too excited that we come out flat. We know you will be there with us and we cannot wait to see all of you.

I have to cut this short as I have to go take a mid-term and answer a few more TV questions! I hope to see you guys on Saturday-should be a special day! Go Blue!

TWO BIG WINS, THE REAL DVR, A SPLASH OF POWDER AND GREAT FANS

What's up everyone?

What a great week! I have so many things to talk about that I'm not sure I will get it all down. BUT ... How about two wins over two really good teams AND the crowds were great for both games – even though one was on the road.

When all is said and done in my Michigan career, Saturday's game against Ohio State will be one of my favorite memories. All the fans showing up at 5 a.m. for ESPN College GameDay, the atmosphere leading up to the game all day and then that game itself. It was and is truly a special moment in my career.

Crisler was so loud that I could not hear anyone talking to me on the bench. Everyone was on the edge of their seats and it was just a great college basketball game. We have a goal of winning a Big Ten championship and the only way to accomplish that was by beating Ohio State at home. We did that.

We couldn't have done it without our great fans and as I tell everyone – we have as good of a home-court advantage as anyone in the country and that's a big reason why we haven't lost there yet.

Now onto a very important matter!

The College GameDay part of the day was very cool to take part in, but I need to clarify some things about who watches what on our DVR from Zack (Novak) and Stu's (Douglass) "Know Your Teammate" interview.

First of all, I only started watching Gossip Girl my freshman year because Zack told me how good of a show it was. I'll admit I got hooked for a while, but this year I stopped watching because I lost interest. Zack, HOWEVER, still watches the show weekly and as he said, he is a big Serena van der Woodson fan, but then again who isn't? The other show we BOTH watch is Keeping up with the Kardashians. I have no comment on that.

I'm sure many of you noticed Zack looked pretty good on College GameDay Saturday morning. Some would say his face was even glowing. Well, the reason his face was glowing was due to the fact that he had a nice little touchup by a makeup artist before he went on TV.

As good of a win Saturday was over the Buckeyes, I'm more impressed with our win Tuesday over Northwestern. All the experts said this was the ultimate let down game and we had no chance of winning. I even had a reporter tell me 10 minutes before the game that we had no shot.

I just smiled because maybe in years past we wouldn't be able to handle success, but this team has great mental toughness and we are playing for a Big Ten championship! Teams don't get a chance to compete for a ring every year, so the excuses about being tired and not focused really weren't an option. We took care of business.

The day before we left for Chicago, Stu said that Northwestern's arena was small and not that loud. Well he was right about it being small, but it was really loud Tuesday night. However, it was loud with chants of "Let's Go Blue!"

That is one of the coolest parts of playing for Michigan. We have such passionate fans and they are everywhere. The entire upper deck of the arena was packed wearing Maize and Blue. After the game, we signed autographs like it was a home game. All in all, it was just a special night for our team.

Now we move onto Senior Night Saturday against Purdue which will be very special and emotional for our fans, team, coaches and me. It should be a great crowd as we continue our push to winning a championship.

Oh yea, don't forget to check out my video feature from Coach Beilein's TV show.

Go Blue!

THE WORK AHEAD, A SHOT AT THE TITLE AND A LITTLE SENIOR DAY

What's up everyone?

We are coming off a great win at Illinois, something a Michigan team has not done in a long time. I believe I was told 1995. That is a long, long time. How about those performances from Tim (Hardaway Jr.) and Trey (Burke)? I mean they impress us more and more as the season goes along.

Now we have just one more to go. We have one more day to get ready for Penn State in what is a huge game for multiple reasons.

For one, with a little help from Ohio State and a win over Penn State, we can be Big Ten champions. It would be a three-team split, but that would not really matter at all to us. All year we have talked about winning a championship and whether it is a tie or outright. It would be a major accomplishment.

A win would also put us over .500 on the road in the Big Ten, which is a sign of a really good team. Go look around the country at how many teams are over .500 on the road in their conference. You will not find many!

After every workout this year, whether it was a weight lifting session in July, an individual with our coaches in September or practice in October, we have ended each session saying "Big Ten champs" on three when we bring it in at the end.

It has been a goal every since we lost to Duke last year to win the best conference in the country and with two days left in the season, we have put ourselves in position to do just that. It would just show what a ton of hard work and focus can really do!

Going back a little, I didn't get to really write about Zack (Novak) and Stu (Douglass) on senior night. Don't worry, I have a lot more to write on them at a more appropriate time because we still have a ton of basketball left, but they deserve some plug in my blog.

There is nothing I can really write that will give them enough credit for what they mean to Michigan basketball. They represent what the program is all about on and off the court. Just think about how much they have improved from their freshman year to now.

Zack could not dribble and get in the lane anywhere like he does now and Stu has become the best perimeter defender in the Big Ten. Just ask Coach Beilein how much improvement he has made. But more importantly, Zack and Stu have been the faces behind the turnaround of Michigan basketball, the ones answering all the questions through the bad times and now the good times.

They have never backed away from any question, any appearances and have represented the program as well as possible. I get so many emails telling me to thank them for all they have done while at Michigan and I share it with them all the time because they deserve to know just how special this turnaround has been.

Lastly, I have received some questions about how we travel for road games. Simply put, we travel like a pro team. All of our flights are chartered meaning we fly with just our team on the plane. We always fly in the night before a game and leave right after usually getting home around 2 a.m. depending on what time the game started and where it was at. Many teams are not as lucky as us and cannot fly privately, so they have to miss school the next day and fly commercial home. Next time I write, hopefully, we are celebrating a championship. Go Blue!

3/5/2012

THE FIFTH ROAD WIN, RACING BACK, THE JOY OF BEING A CHAMPION

WHAT IS UP EVERYONE!

Yesterday will go down as one of the most surreal days of my life. I'm still not exactly sure what happened, but the way it went down was magical. Try and follow below as I explain!

Before I do, don't forget to watch this feature. Big Ten Champs! It will help this blog.

It all started in Happy Valley when we had our typical team meeting around 8:30 a.m. We went over our last-minute keys to the game and knew what this day could bring, but our focus was on doing what we could control in beating Penn State. No one was thinking about the game that was supposed to tip at 4 p.m.

We shot the "you-know-what" out of the ball against them – Evan (Smotrycz) was on fire, Tim (Hardaway Jr.) was not missing, Trey (Burke) was being Trey and Zack (Novak) and Stu (Douglass) continued to show how versatile they have become. We played a really good game and it showed that we were locked in. The goal before the game started was to get over .500 on the road in the Big Ten, we accomplished that.

The game ended around 3 p.m., and we celebrated a great team win. We had no control over the rest of the day, but the scenario was pretty clear and everyone knew it. The typical media and autograph post game sessions occurred at the Bryce Jordan Center, however, they happened a little faster than usual because there was a big game taking place in about an hour that would affect us just a little bit.

Everyone is giving their predictions on the game while on the bus to the airport. Coach Alexander believes in positive energy so he just keeps saying what he wants/believes will happen. The team agrees William Buford is the key to the game for Ohio State. (We ALL know basketball!)

We pull into Happy Valley airport at 3:57 p.m. and turn on CBS in the hangar. The Creighton/Illinois State game is on and everyone is trying to be the last one through security just to see the tip of the Ohio State/Michigan State game.

Of course, the prior game goes into overtime so we don't see the tip in the airport and are left to refresh our phones about a million times before takeoff.

As soon as we get on the plane, we find the CBS sports feed and begin watching on the plane. Nothing good is happening and the plane is pretty silent. (Matt) Vogrich is sitting next to me, Novak behind and everyone else standing around trying to watch from my computer.

The flight attendant comes to tell us to turn off the computer, but we only close the computer three-quarters of the way (hopefully, she isn't reading this) and still watch until our plane is off the ground and into the air.

Eventually the internet goes out and our last update has Ohio State down 14.

I'm refreshing my phone all the time in the air and of course it isn't going to ever work, but I keep trying. Once we are in the air, everyone listens to music or watches a movie; there is no talk of the game. At some point, my phone gets a roaming message from Canada, not sure how, but it updated the score while we were way up in the air. Ohio State was down nine at half, and you could feel the energy in the plain again. We had a chance!

We landed and now phones are being refreshed at ridiculous rates. Every score is yelled out on the plane and people are voicing their opinions on every play (NOTE: I just cannot share that with you, sorry). We race off the plane and onto the bus that will take us back to Crisler. There is 12 minutes left in the game and OSU is down six. We are trying watching the CBS sports feed on the bus, but our internet connection is awful. Vogrich calls a friend and we get updates from him on the phone. The bus isn't exactly moving fast and Novak keeps talking about how he wants to take over and drive the bus NASCAR style and Corey (Person) wants Stu to drive. I want a police escort!

Timing is everything.

Somehow we pull into the PDC at the four minute media timeout with MSU up a couple. The last four minutes went by about as slow as humanly possible. We all watched in the film room, living and dying with every second.

My heart is beating about as fast as possible. Novak has his shirt off. Evan has his hat over his head; he can barely watch. Tim is pacing the hallways. I'm not sure Stu was breathing. Vogrich, well he was being Vogrich. Coach Jordan can barely watch. It was quite the scene.

Many of you saw the game, the two team's trade blows, and with 25 seconds left, OSU has the ball with the score tied. The play has to be called for Buford. He was playing great and as we called it before, he was the key.

After the timeout, they run a hand off and Buford has the ball going left. We all know Buford going left is deadly. He doesn't miss that shot. The ball leaves his hand with about three seconds left and pure, nothing but net OSU is up two with one second left. MSU misses a last-second prayer and the place erupts.

An amazing scene that thankfully was captured on video! I'm dumping water on people. It's a mosh pit in the middle of the office. Corey has taken his shirt off. Everyone is hugging one another. It is the kind of feeling that words can express, but when you have a goal for 11 months that few believe you can achieve and then achieve it, it makes for these magical moments.

It was an emotional hallway. At one point guys had to sit down because it hadn't really set in what had just happened. Coach B hugged every player. It was surreal!

We still have more magical moments to achieve this year, and that feeling yesterday will only push us to work harder. I just want to thank all the fans who have been with us through everything.

This team plays for each other, but we also play for you, so thanks for all your support.

Go Blue!

3/14/2012

THE BIG DANCE, BOUNCING BACK AND VOTE FOR CB

What's up everyone? March Madness is officially underway.

If you somehow haven't heard yet, we got the fourth seed in the Midwest region. This means we will be taking on the Ohio Bobcats on Friday night – 7:20 p.m. on TNT, so set your DVRs. I know they are a very talented team who has a great point guard, but we will be more than ready with four days to get a game plan together. Our coach's work tirelessly on scouting opponents and no one does it better.

Before we get onto the NCAA Tournament, I want to quickly wrap up the one we just played in.

I'm sure many of you are disappointed with how the Big Ten Tournament ended. Trust me we are just as mad; however, just like all year long we have to learn from the loss and turn it into a positive. It is tournament season and it has a different feel to it. The first game of a tournament is always hard to play in. Our young guys, especially Trey (Burke) just getting his feet wet will be key going forward. No team has responded to a loss better than us all year and we need to continue this trend going forward.

Okay back to the Big Dance.

While this year didn't have as much suspense as last, it is still a surreal experience to see your name called on TV. Coach Beilein, who has been to many NCAA Tournaments, was excited as ever for the selection show. This is what he works so hard for and none of us take for granted how magical it is to make the tournament. Only 68 teams get in and we were ranked 13th of all of them!

We are setting up this week just like we did before we played Ohio State at home. We had about a week to prepare for them and have a week to prepare for the Bobcats. We had a great practice on Tuesday, really getting back to a preseason type of feel with great energy on the court.

At this time of the year, there is a fine line between resting people, but at the same time getting ready. Our coaches have found a really good balance between both over the last month. Today will be another day of preparation as we implement more of our game plan for Ohio and then we leave for Nashville.

Tomorrow we practice in front of the public, which is mostly just a shoot around. Some teams put on spectacular dunk show, but I have a feeling you will see a lot more threes from us than your typical team. We will also practice at a local high school tomorrow, which will be our typical day before practice.

We want to make this week as typical as possible even with the different travel schedule. Then we bunker down in our hotel and get ready for the game. There is no looking back now, we know how hard we have worked to get to this point and don't want this special season to end.

On a much more important note, Carlton Brundidge is in his own NCAA Tournament of his own this month. Carleton is in the best names bracket for Sports Nation and we need all of you to vote for him and make sure he advances. I'm not sure how Carlton is a more unique name than Sai (Tummala) or Eso (Akunne), but apparently Carlton Brundidge has a nice ring to it. Carlton is in the UWE BLAB REGIO -VOTE HERE!

Hopefully we see a ton of you in Nashville as there is a big advantage to having a home crowd in a neutral site. Our fans have been amazing all year long and I have no doubt it will continue this weekend!

I will try and update you as much as I can from Nashville and follow me on twitter @ Jbart20 as I will let you know what's going on from there also.

SPECIAL NOTE: I want to wish our trainer John DoRosario as very happy birthday. He wants everyone to know he looks the same now as he did when he was 21. As BA would say, he's conscious!

Go Blue!

3/26/2012

MY BLOG'S SEASON FINALE, SEE YOU SOON OR THIS SUMMER

What's up everyone?

The 2011-12 Michigan men's basketball season will be remembered for so many things, some of which include winning the best conference in the country, traveling to the most prestigious tournament in the country – the Maui Invitational, for the 24 wins and for the four great seniors.

Years from now when I call Zack (Novak) or Stu (Douglass) and talk about this year, we probably won't talk about any of those things. That is because the journey is way more important than the destination. The memories we will share are the laughs we had on the plane, some crazy idea Coach Alexander had, another memorable quote from Coach Jordan; it is everything that happens during the season that makes a team become a team.

We have traveled all across the country spending almost every day together for six months. The hardest part of the season ending is the knowing that this team will never play together again. In the blink of an eye, when the horn went off and zeroes were on the clock, our season was over. That is what makes sports so special; anything can happen at any time and nothing prepares you for the end!

When I decided to come play for Coach Beilein, he asked me why I wanted to be part of this team. I could have received a scholarship to other schools, instead I chose Michigan! I told him I wanted to be a part of something bigger than myself. There is something mythical about being a part of Michigan. There is something special about being a part of a team, where you give everything you have for the greater good of your teammates. It might not result in wins all the time, but more importantly, it will result in lifelong friendships.

The 16 of us ran every sprint together, watched every clip of film together (trust me, that is a lot harder to do than you think) and most importantly, through all the ups and downs, we stood by each other. We didn't make it to a Sweet 16, but that will not for one second take away all the special memories I have with Zack, Stu, Corey (Person) and Ben (Cronin)!

This season started and ended around three people – Zack, Stu and Corey. I have said it before, but all three of them capture exactly what it is to be a Michigan basketball player.

You saw it all year in victory, but you also saw it in the locker room after the game in Nashville. They didn't complain about the refs, the ball not going in or it just not being our game. They gave credit to Ohio and knew for whatever reason, their time had come to an end. It wasn't the way they deserved to go out, but for those three, the only way to really capture what they meant was to win a national championship.

They have done everything else.

One of the memories I will have for the rest of my life is watching every member of our team – from players to coaches to managers – giving our three seniors a hug for all they have done for our team.

From guys who have been around for decades from Coach Beilein to Brian Townsend to Bob Bland, those three guys needed to know how appreciate everyone is for what they did. They made Michigan fans proud again!

I have seen seniors leave before, but it was nothing like this and it shouldn't have been. It was an emotional scene because no one was ready for our season to be over. When the ball tipped at 7:10 p.m., we all expected to be celebrating at 10 p.m., not spending the last moments as a team together.

When I look back at our season, I think a defining moment came in Iowa City. We played our worst game of the season and got crushed by Iowa. We came into the game listening to everyone say how good we were and let it get to our heads. We were worrying about the wrong things, how many points we were scoring, when we would get the next shot, things good teams don't ever think about.

After the game Zack gave a speech that couldn't have been more perfect. He pretty much said if we are going to win this year it was going to be because everyone will 'Control the Controllables.' This means you do things that luck has no effect on. You can't control if you make a shot, but you can make sure you get a loose ball or a rebound.

We know we weren't as talented as some other teams, so we had to win all the dirty categories, the places we could control. Zack summed it up by saying people always say you have four years to play in college, but this team only has one year to play together. It's not the NBA where you can play as long as you want, this season is it. We all decided after that game that we would play for our seniors this year because this team didn't want 2012 to ever end!

That is why this team played so hard every night. The emails I received always point out how fans love watching us play because we play so hard and for each other. The fans are right because that is what we try to do every night. Whether it is J-Mo (Jordan Morgan) jumping over the seats at Indiana for a rebound, Matt (Vogrich) diving and beating everyone on Ohio State for a loose ball, or Zack and Stu both diving for a loose ball against Wisconsin, we always left it on all the court. That leads to great success and that is why 24 times after a game we sang "The Victors" to celebrate a win. It signified that everyone in that locker room was part of the T-E-A-M.

No one can predict the future, and while we are experiencing a transition period right now, it won't change for one second how we play and why we play. This program is back to being a power and it's the job of Matt, Blake (McLimans), Eso (Akunne) and myself to make sure everyone knows what the expectations are for a Michigan basketball player.

The old teach the young in our program, and one thing we have learned is that if you don't have a culture, then it doesn't matter how much talent you have, you will not win. I will promise everyone the culture will be one of Wolverine Excellence!

It all comes back to making sure every player understands Michigan basketball is way bigger than any single individual. From Cazzie Russell to Phil Hubbard to Glen Rice to now Stu and Zack, we are all just blips on the radar.

I want to thank everyone for reading the blog this year and making this season so special. We have the best fans in the country! I will be back next year for my last hurrah, hoping to capture another special season, and who knows, maybe throw in a few updates throughout the offseason and summer months. Workouts have already started for next year as there is no time to rest. I want to thank our SID Tom Wywrot, again, for letting me write this blog.

Until next time ... Go Blue!

THE 2012-13 SEASON

9/7/2012

I AM BACK, QUESTIONS ANSWERED, CHEF HORFORD

What's up everyone?

I am back for yet another year!

I hope you all had a great summer and are getting ready for what should be a very exciting year for Michigan basketball. We started school Tuesday, which means this is the first week we have been able to work out as a team this fall. Up to this point, the focus has been on growing stronger, getting in tiptop shape and honing our skills through our individual workouts.

Since the end of last season, there has been a lot of hype surrounding this team. Coming off winning a Big Ten title and returning so many key players, it is no surprise that so many "experts" expect us to be good.

But the message around the locker room is clear – nothing is guaranteed.

Anyone who has been here during the last three years knows how much hard work has gone into becoming a championship-level program. It is a season-long journey, which started two days ago and hopefully ends sometime in April, but you can't skip steps along the way.

The only way we can be a good team is by putting in the work every day, and I have no doubt that it will be done. We have enjoyed going from being the hunter to the hunted, but our approach will not change one bit in how we build on that success!

Besides people asking me how good this team can be, the question I get asked the most is, "how do the freshmen look?"

The freshmen have been extremely impressive all summer. Most importantly, they are great kids who fit the Michigan culture. Obviously they are extremely talented, with Mitch (McGary) getting rebound after rebound, Glenn (Robinson III) dunking on people, Nik (Stauskas) hitting threes, Caris (LeVert) slashing to the rim and Spike (Albrecht) dropping dimes.

But their ability to learn and pick things up on the fly is what has been most impressive. Playing in the Big Ten as a freshman is no easy task, but all of them are beginning to understand how hard they have to work and what it takes to win games in the toughest conference in the country.

On a much more important note, I have new roommates. With the departure of Zack (Novak) and Stu (Douglass), joining me in the house is Tim (Hardaway Jr.), Jordan (Morgan) and Jon (Horford).

Jon has taken over our beautiful and vast basement. With those three moving in, the amount of stories we should have will be inordinate, but I will start you out with this one.

Jon thinks he is some kind of master chef. He cooks every meal every day – the messes he makes are a whole different story – but when he starts cooking he doesn't really know what he is cooking yet.

He just pulls things out of the fridge and begins making something. It is a sight to see. But the best part of Jon is that he only knows how to make family-size portions. When he cooks these stews, it is enough to serve our entire team, yet Jon is cooking just for himself. I mean, he makes so much food that we don't need to leave the house for a month.

Many of you have to be wondering why Jon doesn't just reduce each of the ingredients he cooks with. Well, he claims if he tries to reduce the size of the meal, he will ruin the proportion of ingredients he has in there. He just doesn't know how to cook for himself.

You may also be asking yourself why we don't just eat some of the food he makes for our dinner and the reason is simple. As I said before, Jon never really knows what he is making until he is done. So I don't trust him enough to make something good enough for my dinner!

Moral of the story, if anyone is hungry and wants to come eat dinner, our house always has a ton of leftovers.

I will continue writing all year as I have done the past couple years. Hopefully, I will see many of you at the football game this weekend as we beat Air Force and start a long winning streak.

Go Blue!

DEFENSIVE FOCUS, MY OWN JERSEY SHORE TAN

What's up everyone?

I hope you are all having a great week after watching our football team pull off a tough win against Air Force. It doesn't matter if you win by 45 or seven, a win is a win. So good job boys!

We are right in the middle of preseason workouts with the excitement of our first practice about a month away. I cannot even believe the season is right around the corner.

This preseason has had a complete new emphasis than in years past. In prior years, we focused a lot of skill work, shooting and passing. This year, we have spent 95 percent of the time on defense – from slides, to being in gaps, to taking charges.

Our goal is to be the best defensive team in the country.

The idea behind spending so much time on defense is simple – we want to get out and run. The only way to run is to get stops on defense. Our defense is going to lead to our offense. If you think about our best wins last year – home against Wisconsin, Purdue on the road and then Michigan State at home – we really got in a stance and locked guys up.

The most exciting part of this process is that the team has completely bought in. The idea of running and gunning is something every player dreams about, and it is showing with how hard everyone is working and the energy in the gym.

Now, I have another story for you. It is a story that really should have been an episode of Seinfeld.

One day this summer in July, with the temperature at like 103 degrees, I decided I wanted to go work on my tan and lay outside – everyone looks better with a nice tan. Our house has a porch off the second floor, which is perfect for lying outside. I knew I wouldn't be able to stay out there long because it was so hot, but I needed some vitamin D.

As I'm lying outside, Jordan (Morgan) comes out to make fun of me saying I should be on the Jersey Shore and tells me that he and Tim (Hardaway Jr.) were going to the mall. They leave. I'm getting a great tan listening to Call Me Maybe and life is good. It gets to that point where I've had enough. I'm dripping in sweat and just want to go back inside to my AC.

That is until I try and go back inside and somehow the door is locked. I'm pulling on the door, turning the knob, but that door isn't opening and its 110 degrees on my phone now. I know for a fact I didn't lock that door, but I know that instinctually Jordan locks every door no matter what the door leads to.

Right away, I know he locked me out! I look down, but the porch is too high to jump off without me breaking something. I'm furious with Jordan and cannot wait to scream at him on the phone for locking me out of my own house. Just one small issue, my phone now says heat warning, and I cannot make any calls.

For a second, I thought that could be it for me, one of the most embarrassing ways for me to die, on my own porch, but at least I would go out really tan. I also was thinking this really would make a great blog entry if I would be around to write about.

About an hour passes by and I'm just baking in the sun. By this point I'm beyond Jersey Shore tan, just as red as a tomato. All the sudden I hear Tim laughing and I begin banging on the door with all the strength I have left (I'm being a little dramatic). Jordan is right behind him and they have the nerve to ask me why I'm sweating so much and tell me that I was outside for too long because now I am burnt.

I'll let you only imagine what I said to both of them. Remember I have to keep things PG in my blog.

Now for a little update on everyone's two favorite people from the state of Indiana – Stu (Douglass) and Zack (Novak). They are both enjoying their times in Spain and Holland, respectively. They are in training camp right now enjoying two-a-days, but also trying to embrace the culture and have some fun. I will try and keep you updated all year on them. In fact, I hear that I will have some blog competition this year as Novak will be penning things from overseas – should be interesting. Just remember who began this whole thing.

With that I hope everyone has a great weekend, with another win for our football team.

Go Blue!

9/28/12

START AROUND THE CORNER, SCHEDULE BREAKDOWN

What's up everyone?

Hope everyone is doing well. The season is fast approaching with less than two weeks until the beginning of practice. We are anxious to really get started and begin the journey of the 97th team in Michigan men's basketball history!

We are still in eight-hour work weeks with only two of those hours devoted to working with our basketball coaches. At this point, we are still only focusing on defense, but we are making strides, especially with our freshmen just understanding our system. The sooner you can pick up rotations and quick man procedures, the sooner you can play!

That leaves six hours a week that we work with Jon Sanderson – our strength and conditioning coach. I truly believe he is the best in the country because everything we do has an emphasis on basketball. You have a lot of strength coaches who believe in this football mentality of lifting as much weight as possible.

We believe in doing things that translate to being stronger, faster and more explosive on the basketball court. It is clear how much more athletic and stronger our team has gotten in the past couple years working with him. It is these six weeks where we really put in the work with him that pays off all season long.

I wanted to talk about this last week, but our official schedule finally came out. While I'm sure fans have certain things they look form like when we play Michigan State and Ohio State, as a player there are things I always look for as well. Now I already know the non-conference schedule so that isn't what I really evaluate, but the first thing I look for is our bye week and when exactly that is.

This year we actually have two one-week byes, which I think is huge. The season is so grueling and exhausting that the ability to rest up for a week, get better as a team and even get a couple days off is so underrated.

You have to remember; the whole season you pretty much spend practice getting ready for other teams. Practicing their offense and running plays you believe will work against them. A bye allows you to practice what you need to work on. We can scout ourselves and work on what Michigan needs to get better at!

The other thing I look at is the amount of back-to-back road games we have in conference. This year the number is two, but only one is on what I call a short turnaround. In years past, that number has been three or four and it is an exhausting process.

For example, let's say we play at Northwestern on Wednesday and at Indiana on Saturday. That means we leave Tuesday night, play on Wednesday and then leave right after the game. Typically we land around 2 a.m., with classes starting seven hours later. On Thursday, we have a light practice then leave again on Friday for Indiana. Obviously, we play Saturday and then fly back landing early Sunday morning. That means we at some point were in the air on Tuesday, Wednesday (after the game), Thursday (early morning 2 a.m.), Friday, Saturday (after the game) and Sunday (early morning 2 a.m.). That is exhausting traveling everyday and having to play! Those are the two main things I look at when evaluating our schedule.

Check out the schedule and come and see us when you can. We hear we could have many sellouts.

Okay, I also want to give myself a shout out, well actually Travis Conlan. There was an article posted that Duke was the first to have iPads for scouting reports and film work. As you know, Travis had that idea for us to go paperless when we first moved into the Davidson Player Development Center. So, I just want to make sure he gets his due. Check it the article (CBS Sports) and the correction. Go Blue! Michigan Blue!

Lastly, I want to congratulate my youngest sister, Kirby, on her Bat Mitzvah. You did a great job and I'm so proud of you!

Have a great weekend and Go Blue!

GETTING LINED UP, MEDIA DAY, THE JOURNEY

What's up everyone?

It is amazing how fast times flies by, but we are officially at the start of the 2012-13 season. We couldn't be more excited about it. We have spent the last five months lifting weights, running, shooting jumpers and playing pickup to get us ready for this day!

The first week I consider our "training camp" – where we really get after it with about two-and-a-halfhour practices. I have a feeling we will spend a ton of time on defense, as that is a staple of Michigan basketball, but I'm sure we will do a ton of competitive drills during the first week.

This is where you see great competition in practice, guys trying to earn minutes. The best part about our team is no matter how fierce the competition gets on the court, it doesn't affect the relationships off of it. We know the harder we work in practice and the more of a battle there is for minutes, the better our team will be. Every team starts practice tomorrow and every team is going to think they are working as hard as anyone in the country. We just need to bring it every day and the rest will take care of itself.

This past Wednesday was our team media day, always some of the guy's favorite day of the year. Knowing my new roommates, what this means to me is that guys are going to have to get "lined up" – AKA getting a haircut so they look great for the camera.

I would have bet a lot that our downstairs bathroom would turn into a barbershop. Sure enough it did. I got home from the store and there was Tim (Hardaway Jr.) with a huge smile on his face getting lined up. Just to be sure for all of you, I did not sit in the chair. I could only imagine what they would do.

Media Day was a success for sure. It is always cool to see the freshmen wide-eyed with all the media attention and answering the same questions over and over. I thought they all did a great job and answered the questions just like a Michigan Man should. I had someone ask me a very interesting question, "Does it ever seem like the whole season doesn't mean too much because you know it just comes down to March Madness?"

It seems people forget or don't realize that the best part of the season is the journey.

Now, yes it is great to win Big Ten championships and make the NCAA Tournament, but just as special are the laughs we share in the locker room, on the team plane or at the hotel. The journey is what makes the season mean so much and all the memories with it. So I would never trade just getting to March with a No. 4 seed like last year, because the moments starting tomorrow and ending in March are what the ride is all about!

I will write again in a week, when a lot of guys are banged up and tired from a week of training camp, but it is amazing how much we will learn and how far we will come in that short time. With our first game about three weeks away, there is not a lot of time like other years to prepare.

Good luck to the football team this weekend. It should be a great Homecoming weekend. Go Blue!

BIG WIN, BIG MEN DOWN LOW, BIG SWAG

What's up everyone?

Nothing like writing a blog after watching our football team beat State! Wow, what a game by both teams. We fought to the end and Brendan Gibbons was clutch as always. When you hear about how hard our football team works and how much that game meant to them, it is awesome to see them pull off the win. The Paul Bunyan trophy is home!

Our team isn't doing too badly, either. After about a week of practices, we are right where I would expect us to be. The competition has been great, practices super intense and as always a ton of coaching. We have been scrimmaging quite a bit to get used to playing with each other. Some of the improvements guys have made are just incredible. It is more evident in sports than anything else, but hard work really does pay off. We had guys in the gym all spring and summer working for this time right now.

Two guys I want to really point out are Jon Horford and Jordan Morgan. Both guys are gym rats, always getting up jumpers, working on their post moves and their ball handling. In the first week of camp those two have really played great basketball. Rebounding, finishing around the basket, passing, pretty much everything you want out of a big guy, those two guys have shown. I get so many emails telling me we need to play bigger. Well this year you just might see that because those guys are showing they deserve to be on the court.

The talent is there no doubt about it, now it is all about having this team come together and play defense. If we can play team defense, get back in transition and rebound this team can do something special. The Big Ten is loaded as always but I love what I see and how hard the team is working. Our first game is in less than two weeks and I think you guys are going to love what you see!

Now onto a matter I have meant to blog about for a while, but now is the perfect time.

I'm not one to complain because we at Michigan get amazing gear, but I'm convinced Coach (LaVall) Jordan has his own adidas contract. I'm talking along the lines of Derrick Rose, and now Justin Bieber – Coach Jordan has stuff NO ONE else has.

From shoes to sweats to sweaters to v-necks, adidas doesn't sell his stuff in stores. Coach already has a ton of swag, but his exclusive gear he has pushes it over the top. I should point out that all the stuff he has is "so fresh" as Corey (Person) would say. Coach Jordan just replies he has a "guy." If anyone knows who this "guy" is please write in to the blog because I need to know him.

Again congrats to our football team and our seniors, I know guys like Denard Robinson and Jordan Kovacs really wanted this one, along with all of you.

Go Blue!

SOMEONE NEW, VIDEO GAME MADNESS, SQUAD 96

What's up everyone?

Four days!

That's all that is left before we tip off the 2012-13 season with our first exhibition game Thursday night (Nov. 1) against Northern Michigan. It seems like an awfully long time since we played Ohio at the NCAA Tournament. I do know this – we can't wait to start playing against other teams. We are at that point in the preseason where you are sick of playing against each other and want to face a real opponent.

The other thing that is very exciting is the reopening of Crisler Center. It looks like a completely new arena, and that combined with the WDPDC makes our facilities better than anyone else in the country. Our fans are going to be 'amaized' – get it – walking into it because nothing looks the same.

Our team has made a ton of progress in two short weeks of practice. We are still learning and teaching new things every day, but you can see improvements being made. From our defensive principles to running coach Beilein's four-guard offense, everything is beginning to come together.

While we have focused a ton on defense, now is the time we try and get the crispness of the offense down. The special thing about his offense is that it's all based off reading the defense. So many teams you see run play after play, we rarely run plays and as coach says, "just play ball!"

As a player that is all you could ever ask, there is nothing predetermined, simply just play basketball and read your defender. Now that we have added a ton of ball screens and opened it up even more, I'm not sure there is a better offense for a skilled offensive player.

Off the court, NBA 2k13 has taken over our locker room. That video game is being played 24/7. From what I understand, Trey (Burke) and Caris (LeVert) are the two best players on the team, with Eso (Akunne) closing in.

Some of you might be saying we need to spend less time playing video games and more time on the court, but Trey has stated he has actually learned moves from playing the game. I actually have seen Trey use the euro step more in two weeks than all last year and he is saying some of that is from the video game. You never know where you will learn something new.

With that, hopefully I see a ton of you Thursday night. Squad 96 will take the court for the first time as a team. While you get four years of eligibility at U-M, this team will only be together for one special year.

That is the point we make in the locker room all the time – leave it all out there for each other, for the seniors because you are only guaranteed so many games. I can't guarantee how many games we will win, but I can guarantee will play our hearts out and represent this school the way it should, like leaders and the best!

Have a great week! Again, we hope to see you Thursday! Go Blue!

11/5/12

BEING CAPTAIN, MAKING A GRETZKY, COMIC RELIEF

What's up Wolverine Nation? Yea, I thought I would change it up a bit.

Not a bad weekend to be a Michigan fan, with the football team pulling off a big win Saturday (Nov. 3) at Minnesota and keeping the Little Brown Jug, and of course us taking care of business on Thursday night (Nov. 1) against Northern Michigan. It was a great team effort with so many people contributing.

While I don't want to write too much about me being named captain, I just want to say how much of an honor it is. Being selected at a school like Michigan is something I value greatly.

My job is actually easy with all the great leadership we already have in our locker room. Guys like Matt (Vogrich), Jordan (Morgan), Corey (Person), Eso (Akunne), Blake (McLimans), Tim (Hardaway Jr.) and Trey (Burke) do an outstanding job already leading and nothing is going to change. The only difference is I get the privilege of shaking hands with the referees before games and will have the opportunity to talk to Teddy Valentine and Ed Hightower, two fan favorites.

Okay let's get back to the team. While, obviously, we still have a ton to work on and clean up, the thing I took away from the game was how well we passed to ball. When you have a lot of talent, there is a tendency to hold onto the ball and be a little selfish.

Not with this team – the ball was constantly swinging from side to side and putting the defensive in close-outs. We track something called a "Gretzky" pass. Simply put, it is the pass that leads to the assist. This pass is so important because it puts the defensive at a disadvantage quickly.

For example, when we run a pick-and-roll and Spike (Albrecht) quickly swings it out after being doubled team, we are now playing with a 4-on-3 advantage. Our goal on offense is to get these advantages because you are just one pass away from scoring now. On Thursday night, you saw this scenario over and over.

The big question I have for you is... How about Crisler Center?

I wasn't joking when I said there were no words to describe it. For people who didn't make it out Thursday night, from what I hear you better get your tickets soon and come check out this team and the arena. Tickets are being bought at historic rates and we want a full house every time we play. Don't miss out on this team!

And now for your comic relief...

I get to tell another story about myself. Yesterday, I was trying to do laundry (already the first problem in this story), which is located in our basement and also serves as (Jon) Horford's living quarters. All the lights were off, so I figured he was taking a nap since we just finished practice about an hour ago.

With me being the nice guy that I am, I didn't want to wake him up so I left the lights off in the pitch black basement and figured I could feel my way to finding the storage room where the washer is located. I have lived in the same place for three years so you would think I have a feel for it by now.

I make it down all the stairs and figure I'm home safe with a big smile on my face. As soon as I relax, BAAM! I walk right into the storage room door. Unfortunately for me, I didn't win this battle and crushed my head. I now have a huge bump on my head and a lot less self-pride. I then had to turn the lights on because I was a little dazed and of course Horford was not even downstairs. Yep, he wasn't even there. I had the lights off for no reason.

I will write again next week after we play two more games and really get this thing started. Come out and cheer us on! Again, I really am honored to be Team 96's captain. I really appreciate all the kind words everyone has said to me!

Have a great week and Go Blue!

11/19/12

POSSESSIONS, TIM'S 1,000, MICHIGAN SQUARE GARDEN

What's up everyone?

It has been a while since I last wrote and a lot has happened! We went 2-0 in the regional games for the NIT Season Tip-Off, knocking off IUPUI and Cleveland State – two very well-coached mid-major teams. Because we won, we now head to New York on Tuesday to play in the championship rounds at Madison Square Garden. I cannot tell you how excited we are to get out there and play in front of all our East Coast fans!

Before I talk about New York, I need to recap our two performances last week.

What I was most impressed again about was how we moved the basketball and played so unselfish. It was a thing of beauty to see all the extra passes being made. The other key I believe has been our improved rebounding. We talk about it all the time – getting those extra possessions. Turning the ball over is losing a possession and getting an offensive rebound is creating an extra one. So far, we have been doing a terrific job of taking care of the ball and cleaning the ball off the glass

You have to give a ton of credit to Jordan (Morgan), Jon (Horford) and Max (Bielfeldt) for the time they spend in the weight room this summer with Coach (Jon) Sanderson. There is no doubt those three are stronger and more explosive. Then you add in guys like Mitch (McGary) and Glenn (Robinson III), who naturally find ways to just go get the ball and it makes us a very good rebounding team. We need to keep this up all year long.

The other guy I need to give a huge shout out is Tim (Hardaway Jr.). Not only for scoring 1,000 career points, an amazing accomplishment in which he basically did in two years, but how much more of a complete player he has become.

Tim worked extremely hard this summer on his ball handling so he could become a play maker and no doubt he has become one. Add in that he has become an elite defender and is pulling down rebounds at an alarming rate. He definitely has us playing better. Tim knows the more diversified his game is, the better our team is. I couldn't be happier for all the success he his having because people that work as hard as Tim deserve to be rewarded!

Okay, on to New York.

We cannot wait to play Pitt on Wednesday night (Nov. 21) at 9:30 p.m. on ESPN. We have had a week to rest and prepare and the team is itching to get back into action. I have heard now for a week how Madison Square Garden turns into Michigan Square Garden when we play there. So the challenge is out there. I want to walk out Wednesday night and see Maize and Blue filling up that place.

I want to wish everyone a very happy Thanksgiving! Have a great week and make sure to catch us in action as we try and capture our first championship of the season!

Oh, and also to the football team Beat Ohio and Go Blue!

THE BIG APPLE, THE TITLE, THE CONFIDENCE, THE ELEVATOR

What's up everyone?

I certainly hope you all had a great Thanksgiving. I know we did, spending a week together in Times Square and winning an NIT championship.

Our first road trip as a team was a huge success. Anytime you play on the road and stay in a hotel, it is an adjustment especially for the freshmen. All five of them did a great job of adjusting to not sleeping in your own bed and all the little things that can be a distraction. This is a very good sign moving forward.

I loved the way our team played in those two games against Pittsburgh and Kansas State. The first thing that needs to be talked about is our team rebounding and toughness. We wanted to be beasts on the boards and win the battle on the glass. Our big men deserve a ton of credit for boxing out and our guards for going in there and cleaning it up. When we watch film, the best rebounds are the ones where the ball hits the floor and then we clean it up because that means everyone is being boxed out. We saw that multiple times this week. If we can sustain this all year, good things will happen going forward!

The next guy who needs a mention is Nik (Stauskas), who plays with a ton of confidence; he truly believes that every time he touches the ball, he is going to put it in the basket. Most freshmen on the big stage like he was this week would show some nerves but not Nik. He just played basketball, knocked down jumpers and got to the basket. While some label Nik just as a shooter, he is a terrific passer who can get to the basket as well. As he continues to learn and get better on both sides of the basketball, Nik will be a real weapon and game changer.

Most importantly, the best part of the week was how many people we had contribute. Jon (Horford) played big minutes on Friday, Spike (Albrecht) was huge in giving Trey (Burke) a rest and Mitch (McGary) dominated the glass! We want to be relentless with our depth and you saw an example of this Friday night, where we kept guys fresh and on the attack!

Being in Times Square is definitely an experience. From seeing the Naked Cowboys in the street to seeing a floating Snoopy in the Thanksgiving Day Parade, the lights are always on and people are always on the street. It truly is a city that never sleeps.

The funniest story of the week goes to my man Mitch. We had a shootaround before our game Wednesday night and as everyone was boarding the bus to head to the Garden, we noticed one person was missing.

As we walked out of the hotel lobby, we noticed these firemen walking inside with huge axes. Corey (Person) joking around as usual said, 'I would hate to be the person they are about save.'

Sure enough, it was Mitch who was stuck in an elevator with 13 other people. Now Mitch is a big guy so being stuck is already not fun, but with 13 people smothered around you, that is really not a good scenario. To make it even worse, there were children crying in the elevator for all 40 minutes while he was stuck. Luckily, the firemen didn't have to use the ax and Mitch made the bus in time! I can guarantee Mitch will never forget this first road trip as a member of the Wolverines!

Now we move on to a very good N.C. State team who no doubt is looking to come into Crisler Tuesday and get a big win. We need to be able to handle success and not prepare any differently. I'm very confident this team will remain hungry and nothing will change in our preparation. I'm also very confident Crisler will be rocking Tuesday night and it will be a special atmosphere.

I will see you all Tuesday night.

Go Blue and have a great week!

12/7/12

TWO MORE WINS, NICE SUITS, JUSTIN BIEBER

What's up everyone?

We have played a couple games since I last wrote. Both were good wins! The constant throughout the year and especially those two games were great team efficiency. We are taking great team shots, making the extra pass and really locking down on the defensive end.

Last Saturday we played our first road game of the year at Bradley. It was an extremely hostile environment and something our young team needed to experience. It was also a very cool experience for Max (Bielfeldt), as he got to play in his hometown.

One thing is very clear, Peoria, Ill. loves Max. He was like the President – every single person at the game wanted to say hi to him no matter which team they were cheering for. The ovation Max got when he entered the game was louder than maybe anything else that happened that day! The Bielfeldt family even got us "Peoria" themed goodie bags so thanks to them for being great hosts!

Max played great, as he has been really coming along and making improvements every day. The Moose, as we call him, is going to make a big impact here as he continues to learn and work hard. Jordan (Morgan) also played a great game, recording a double-double. When J-Mo is active, our team is really hard to beat. There are not many big men who are as athletic as he is, or that can run the court with him and hedge ball screens. That inside presence is something we need every game.

Many people have been asking why I keep wearing suits on the sideline. Unfortunately, I had ankle surgery last week and will be out for about two months. It is my third surgery on that ankle, but hopefully the third time is the charm.

With being hurt, now I get to show off my suit game. I have a lot of competition with both Coach (Bacari) Alexander and Coach (LaVall) Jordan who have won the best-dressed assistant award, but I'm ready for the challenge. I'm going to take a lot of pride in this!

Our last game was against a very solid Western Michigan team. The biggest challenge with them was guarding their pick-n-roll and high-low game. Western runs some really good sets and after about the first 10 minutes we really locked down on the defensive end. The key to stopping Western, and pretty much every team in college basketball, is getting people on the help line. As long as we have people stay "hot" as we call it, our defensive it going to be just fine.

The other key to our success has been the play of our point guard. Everyone knows Trey (Burke) can score with the best of them, but what has really stood out this year has been his ability to make other players better. In our last two victories, Trey has 18 assists and zero turnovers. No one in the country is touching that. It goes way beyond the numbers as well – Trey just completely controls the game and you can tell our team really looks up to him. His growth as a leader this year has been huge and when one of your best players is always talking, it makes your team better!

Lots of people are making a big deal about our five freshmen now all playing minutes. For one, they are all extremely talented and playing well, but I hope people appreciate how much some of the veterans are helping them out.

For example, Matt (Vogrich) has done an incredible job with helping Nik (Stauskas). We have so many plays and so many reads, but you can always see on our bench Matt talking to Nik and giving him directions. We always talk about being unselfish on the court, but our team is special because we don't care who gets the credit as long as it helps the team.

On another note, there is much buzz around our team with the Justin Bieber love.

Before everyone goes and gives Nik and Mitch (McGary) all the Bieber love, I much point out I was rocking his music long before those two stepped on campus, just ask Zack (Novak) and Stu (Douglass). I, however, will never sing on the jumbotron like Mitch did.

I will give Mitch credit for having a pretty good voice. Mitch's talent goes way off the basketball court and he actually is a great opera singer. He sings in the hot tub all the time and he can almost break the glass!

I cannot wait to see our sellout crowd this Saturday. As you know, we want all of you there as early as you can. I think doors open an hour and half before the game. Our fan support this year has been great and we need the crowd to get there early so Crisler is rocking when we take the court.

It is an exciting time for Michigan basketball and you don't want to miss out!

And as always, Go Blue!

BROOKLYN, ALUMS, BURNING BACON, BREAKFAST IN BED

What's up everyone?

We are getting ready to take on Eastern Michigan tonight, our last game before we head on Christmas break. Eastern is a very talented team, which plays a trapping 2-3 zone we need to attack. They have already defeated Purdue this year, and we know how good they are. It should be a great game, and I'm looking forward to seeing Crisler packed tonight like always.

Last weekend, we played a good West Virginia team in Brooklyn, N.Y., and pulled out a hard-fought win. West Virginia is very physical, just like a typical Big Ten team, and we matched them with our toughness. I thought Trey (Burke) was just sensational, pushing the ball up the court and just making everyone on the court better. When Trey and Tim (Hardaway Jr.) get everyone involved and are still able to score, our team is going to be hard to beat.

The most impressive part of our trip to Brooklyn was our fans. It might have said neutral-site game on the schedule, but the Barclays Center was as loud as the Crisler Center.

We love playing in New York because of our fans.

I was also fortunate enough to get to talk to many donors and fans at a pregame reception in the Barclays Center.

Along with Dave Brandon, it was great to meet so many U-M fans who love our school. It is pretty special to see so many people love the Block 'M' and unite over it. The excitement around our team is amazing, but more than anything else, fans love the way our team plays. We take pride in being unselfish, being together and having fun. I promise nothing is going to change regarding that all year long.

Off the court, there has been some controversy in our house.

My cooking skills, or I should say lack of skills, is the issue. It all started because Tim set off our smoke detector by cooking some bacon. It woke me up from a great sleep, and I came downstairs to see our kitchen full of smoke. Luckily, nothing happened to Tim or the bacon. However, since I was making fun of Tim, he and Jordan (Morgan) said they had never seen me cook since we had lived together and didn't think I could make anything, even something as easy as scrambled eggs.

Now I'm no top chef, but I mean making scrambled eggs is pretty simple. My point is it doesn't take a genius to make scrambled eggs, so I was pretty offended they thought so little of me. So to put this all to bed, I offered to make all of them eggs for breakfast and serve it to them in their bed. I can even throw in some cheese if they prefer it. Because of our finals schedule, I have yet to make the eggs, but I promise I can and will prove no one makes a better scrambled egg than me. I learned from the best, my mom! As proof I might even send some photos.

I want to wish everyone a very happy holiday.

I hope you all spend some quality time with your families and I know our team is looking forward to going home for a couple days and getting a nice break. Hopefully, I see many of you tonight. Go Blue!

QUALITY TIME, THE MONSTER, SECRET SANTA

What's up everyone?

I hope you all had a great holiday. I know our team enjoyed the break and being able to spend some quality time with our families. We don't get to spend a lot of time at home, so we definitely cherish every second when we are with them!

Before we talk about our break, I want to recap our win against Eastern Michigan. We played very well on both sides of the court and really shared the ball on the offensive side. This has been something that is becoming a regular occurrence and that is so great to see.

The key guy I want to point out against Eastern was Mitch (McGary). Mitch is one of the hardest workers on our team, spending countless extra hours working on his game. We see how much better he is getting, but for him to win Big Ten Freshman of the Week and record a double-double in the second half is just proof how good he can be. We call him the "Monster" because of how relentlessly he goes after the ball, and when he wants to get it, Mitch is going to get the ball. Mitch is just going to continue to get better and better, which is a scary thought considering how good he is now!

Now back to that great three-day break.

For the first time in a long time, it gives everyone a reprieve from basketball. Since the week school started, we have pretty much been going hard five to six days a week. You don't realize just how tired your body is until you're home for a couple days. Now that we are back and have had a couple practices under our belt, you can feel the excitement in the gym for the second half of our season. I think guys reflected over the break a little bit and know if we continue to get better and work hard, Team 97 can be special!

We are now preparing for our game against Central Michigan this Saturday. The game is a sellout, and we cannot wait to play in front of our amazing fans. For the rest of the season, we need to create as big of a homecourt advantage as possible and that means packing as many people into Crisler as possible. When teams walk out of their tunnel and see maize all over the place, it is extremely intimating. Central Michigan is a very talented team that can really shoot the ball and plays well in transition. We are going to have to be on point defensively and getting back on defense.

Oh, I almost forgot, I have another off-the-court doozy for you.

When we got back from our break, we had a team "white elephant" party. For those who don't know what it is, well, basically it's a version of Secret Santa but you don't know who is going to get your gift. Some of the funnier gifts were Spike (Albrecht) receiving headphones that would have been cool in the 1970s from Corey (Person). I mean really, they had to be from the '70s! They were what you would call "vintage."

Jordan (Morgan) got a tie that I truly hope he never wears out in public, and Corey got a lantern; since he goes camping so much it will come in handy. However, that is a joke, because Corey has never, and I can safely say will never, go camping. Caris (LeVert) got the best gift of the night, picking up a $25 gift card. I'm not even sure how to explain what I got besides it won't be used. I don't even want to spend the time telling you what it is but would love to hear your guesses. I'm looking forward to seeing many of you Saturday night in Crisler. Go Blue!

1/7/2013

TWO BIG WINS, BIG MITCH, THE CHAMPIONSHIP

What's up everyone?

Not a bad week to be a Michigan basketball fan! We had two tough Big Ten games and two really good wins. We took care of business in the opener at Northwestern in front of a great crowd (there was more maize than purple) and then Iowa at home in front of another sellout crowd!

I personally love playing at Northwestern because of the huge turnout we get from all the Michigan alumni. I have to admit, a lot of my family and friends are there so that makes it special. We had chants of "Let's Go Blue!" and "Defense" the whole game. It really is cool to feel like the home team during an away game.

The most impressive thing about our win there was our ability to lock in on Northwestern with such a young team. They run a unique offense that if you don't focus and communicate, you will be exposed. I had a really good feeling going into the game because of the way we had been practicing. Add that with our transition offense and a great game by Trey (Burke) and Jordan (Morgan) and you get a great road win. Wins on the road are very difficult to come by and to start 1-0 is terrific. J-Mo has really improved his offensive game, which opens up so much for our team!

We got back from Northwestern around 1 a.m. on Friday morning and two days later took on Iowa at home. That is a very quick turnaround especially when playing a game at noon; however, we had two great days of practice and played well again. The thing that was so impressive to me about the Iowa win was just how much fun we had playing together. It is something that has been pretty evident all year, but our unselfishness is what is making this team unique. You see everyone with a smile on their face because we are playing the right way and taking pride in each other's success. Our bench is pretty much standing the whole game!

I thought the guy who changed this game was Mitch (McGary). His energy and effort was contagious to our whole team and made us go on that huge run. The other thing that is pretty evident with all our big guys, but especially Mitch, is when they get clean rebounds, we are really dangerous running. Mitch has such great vision of the court for a big guy and it opens up the whole court!

With all those positives, we still have a ton to work and improve on. We will be right back in the film room tomorrow working on getting ready for Nebraska and making our team better. You do not win any trophies for being good at the beginning of January. This is a long process and the teams that can win and still evaluate their weaknesses will be standing at the end!

Okay, okay, switching gears.

In addition to our game with Nebraska, we have a huge game tomorrow night.

Tomorrow is the championship of our video game tournament. We were all divided into three teams, the freshmen, the seniors and then everyone else (I'll call them the middle men). We had a round-robin tournament playing FIFA and NHL.

Now this was funny because no one on our team really plays these games besides Max (Bielfeldt), who somehow lost to Corey (Person) in what is a bigger upset then the Wizards beating the Heat. After all the dust settled, the seniors will take on the "Middle Men" tomorrow night on the big screen at Crisler Center in a game of NBA 2K!

My team, the seniors, had practice tonight and is ready to go. We know the key is to slow down Trey as he is the key to the "Middle Men." We couldn't be less worried about Tim (Hardaway Jr.), Jon (Horford), Jordan and Max.

It should be noted that I really shouldn't be talking because I'm awful at video games, but at least I admit it unlike some people who live in my house not mentioning names. Eso (Akunne) is our go-to guy and I couldn't be more confident we will pull this one out!

Stay tuned to Twitter because I'm sure there will be a lot of updates/trash talk going on.

With that hopefully I will see many of you Wednesday night. It is going to be another sellout and trust me you don't want to miss out on the action right now!

I want to wish you all a Happy New Year as well!

Go Blue!

BREAKING DOWN FILM, KEYS TO WIN, VOTE NOW!

What's up everyone?

I hope you all had a great weekend besides our little setback. However, we are ready to move on to Minnesota as we have a huge game tomorrow night. Minnesota is a great team and the atmosphere is going to be electric in the barn. Throw in Dick Vitale doing the game and you have what should be a pretty special Thursday night match-up!

To recap what happened at Ohio, we had a very rough first eight minutes, but after that, we closed a 21point gap to three. On the road, you can't spot teams points like that. A lot of credit has to go to them for forcing us to turn the ball over, but it was the first true Big Ten road game for our young team and this will be a huge stepping stone for us going forward.

You always feel awful after the game, until you watch the film and realize how close we were to winning. There are so many plays we want back, but the key to winning on the road in the Big Ten is valuing every possession. You never know which play is going to be the one you want back!

Unlike college football, you don't have to wait a whole week to get another shot on the court. We get another top-10 road test Thursday and if we learn from our mistakes, the outcome will be in our favor.

A big part of Minnesota is its offensive rebounding.

The Gophers lead the conference in creating extra opportunities for themselves. We need to hit a man and box out on every possession. Now there is a good part about teams that really attack the glass. Once we get that rebound, we can get out in transition and run. We want to get down the court in four seconds every time we get the ball, but you can only run when you get stops and get clean rebounds. That is why in practice this week a huge emphasis has been on hitting people early and hard! It's going to be a great game!

Off the court, I am very proud to announce the seniors won our team video game tournament. We pulled off a great NBA 2K win over the sophomores and juniors. Eso (Akunne) clinched the game in the fourth with some really clutch shooting, but the game ball has to go to Blake (McLimans) for getting us a 10-point lead in the first quarter.

Now Blake has never played the game before, so getting a 10-point lead against someone must mean the guy he was playing against was pretty bad. Not trying to put anyone on blast, but (number 52, aka J-Mo) did not come ready to play when the lights were on and everyone was watching. I tend to think it was probably just the experience of the seniors that those young guys couldn't match!

Lastly and most important, coach Beilein has made a habit of making sure we understand how important giving back is. Right now, coaches throughout the country are in a contest to raise money for their favorite charity. We need all our great fans to go to ESPN.com and vote. It only takes a minute to vote and the St. Louis Center of Michigan is a great place that is special to coach!

Make sure you guys all tune in to ESPN Thursday night at 7 p.m. We are ready to get that bad taste out of our mouth and move on Have a great rest of the week and Go Blue!

THREE BIG WINS, JON & MAX, NO. 1

What's up everyone?

It has been a little bit since I last wrote, but our schedule has been absolutely crazy between school, traveling and playing games. A ton has happened and we have played some really good team basketball during the last 10 days!

We have won three games since I last wrote, at Minnesota, against Purdue and then at Illinois. Coach Beilein always says you remember those road wins more than anything else because you have 15,000 people screaming at you at the top of their lungs and we are all we got!

Teams that win a Big Ten championship find ways to win on the road and that is what we are doing right now. It isn't always going to be pretty, but you have to lock down on defense and grind it out.

I'll break down the Illinois game, since it was our most recent win. A couple things really stuck out at me. Jon (Horford) and Max (Bielfeldt) stepped up once Jordan (Morgan) went down with a sprained ankle. We have a saying, "Next Man Up" when someone goes down and those two guys did a great job of stepping up. We see how hard they work in practice every day and how good they really are, but doing it in a game and helping our team get a huge win is extremely rewarding for them.

Max is a guy who has been dominant at practice at times and for him playing at Illinois is a home game in front of all his friends and family, so we were all excited for him. In my opinion, the most impressive thing about Max was his mental toughness. Max airballed his first free throw, but for him to come back and then swish the next two shows how mentally tough he is. A lot of guys would not be able to step up and move past the air ball. It was an easy choice who was going to sing the fight song after the game and as a team we couldn't have been happier for him!

I know everyone wants to know what the No. 1 ranking means to us. For our fans, they can walk around with their heads high and chests out, but for us it doesn't mean a whole much. Coach Beilein made a great point. Do you have any idea who was ranked No. 1 last year at the end of January?

The goal is not to be ranked No. 1 now, but in April. However, the message I will send to our team is that what we are doing is working. The hard work, team thoughts, and everyone buying in – is a recipe for success. If we continue to stay on this path and continue to improve every day, it shows this team can be special!

Off the court, we filmed a behind-the-scenes show for CBS Sports Network this past week. They followed us everywhere for about four days, from going to Mott's Children's Hospital (one of my favorite things to do as a U-M athlete), to me cooking eggs and proving all my doubters wrong. I have always wondered how the Kardashians do it with cameras following them around everywhere. Well I never thought I would utter these words, but I have a newfound respect for them – in that aspect ONLY!

I look forward to seeing many of you at Crisler Wednesday night as we take on Northwestern. The louder the game gets, the more it helps us!

2/7/2013

X FACTOR, TIM'S BIG NIGHT, 80 DEGREES!

What's up everyone?

Wow, yesterday's game against Ohio State was a pretty special day. You – our fans – deserve a ton of credit. The Crisler Center was as loud as I have ever heard it, and we had a huge home court advantage. Everyone that was there got their money's worth because they witnessed a classic Big Ten battle.

I know we had to take it to an extra period, but in the end we were able to come out on top! Check off another top-10 win on our résumé.

I knew it was going to a special day when I pulled up to Crisler at around 11 a.m. and there was already a line for our student section. It stretched all the way from the top of the Mortenson Plaza down the football tunnel stairs. I know it energized us just seeing that. We were able to stop by after our walk through, around 5 p.m., and bring pizzas. I tell you what the crowd must have tripled in size. It was so amazing.

When we got up there, the tent was rocking with live music. You could just feel the buzz for the game in the tent, and it carried over to game time. It was quite the sight. We hope to see the Maize Rage repeat its energy over our last four home games.

Back to the game.

It really came down to Tim (Hardaway Jr.) making big shot, after big shot, after big shot, after big shot. Yep that is four in a row just like in the game. It was one of those nights Tim will never forget for the rest of his life, knocking off the Buckeyes and catching on fire knocking down six long-range buckets.

When things weren't looking real good, Tim showed the kind of leader he is and stepped up. He was just so locked in before the game, I wasn't surprised he had the type of night he did. For me, personally, I couldn't be happier for Tim. He works incredibly hard, and he deserves nights like that!

However, playing in the Big Ten, you cannot really soak in the glory of the win for long.

We now move on to playing Wisconsin on the road, historically one of the toughest places to play in the country. The key to beating the Badgers is just being solid. We cannot beat ourselves taking bad shots or going for steals. They are known for holding the ball for all 35 seconds and making you guard them for the entire shot clock. If you take a second off or don't box out, you are going to get burned. I know by the time Saturday comes around, we will have a terrific game plan in place!

Off the court, our house is having some major temperature issues. It is either too cold or too hot in our house. For example, two days ago I woke up at 6 a.m. sweating. It literally was hard to breathe because it was so hot. I walked downstairs figuring the temperate was at like 75 degrees, but nope, someone set it to 80!!! That is insane and crazy and probably not healthy for you.

After unleashing an investigation, I came to the conclusion Jon (Horford) was cold in his basement, so he just decided to put it up to 80! This comes weeks after Tim set the temperature at 63, where I slept in gloves and a hat.

So I have decided to take things into my own hands and buy a case for our thermostat, and therefore I'm able to lock it and enable no one but myself to control the house temperature! I didn't think it would ever come to this, but I need to sleep comfortably and right now that isn't happening.

Make sure you tune in Saturday and watch us take on the Badgers. Have a great rest of the week. Go Blue!

SMALL MARGIN FOR ERROR, PRACTICE, BIG REUNION

What's up everyone?

I know it has been a tough week for our fans and trust me we aren't happy with what transpired at Michigan State either. However, every team in the country goes through some adversity. It is a good thing it's happening now and not in four weeks when the NCAA tournament starts!

The thing you have to understand about college basketball is how hard it is to win any single game. Your margin for error, especially in the Big Ten is extremely small. When we got off to a 16-0 start, everything looked very easy. No doubt we were playing great basketball, but I could have guaranteed you we were going to have to go through a tough stretch at some point.

Most teams face their first bit of adversity in November or December, but ours didn't come until the middle of February. This is what makes college basketball so great. You need to bring you 'A' game every time you take the court. We know we have to get better and I have no doubt we will!

The other thing worked in our favor is over the next 10 days, we finally have time to really practice. We just went through a grueling stretch playing something like eight games in 23 days. Between having to take off days and just resting your body, there is not a lot of time to get OUR team better.

Most practices are spent preparing for the next opponent. After the State game on Tuesday, we had one of our best practices of the year. It was hard, physical, tough and defensive minded. We got back into that training camp mode and went at each other.

No excuses need to be made for what took place Tuesday night.

We played poorly and give State a ton of credit. But State still has to come back to Crisler and we are going to be more than ready. All of our team goals are still in front of us and our goal now is to just keep getting better because the stretch run is right around the corner. I tell the guys all the time this is going to be the best six weeks of our lives coming up and the memories we make will be forever. Nothing has changed my mind on that front!

Now moving onto to Sunday, it should be a pretty special weekend.

We are dedicating Crisler Center and hundreds of former players will be in town. From Cazzie Russell to Jimmy King to Glen Rice to Zack Novak, who I am sure you saw at the MSU game already. I'm excited for them to see all the new facilities as we now have better facilities than anyone in the country.

However, I'm more excited for all the former players to see how far the program has come and meet our team. Our coaches tell us all the time how former players text them and say how proud they are watching us play because we play so hard and together. We are one big family and it will be great to spend the weekend together.

With that, I hope to see many of you at Crisler Sunday. We are back at home and I know we can't wait to play in front of our fans. I see there is supposed to be a "Stripe Out" for our game. If you, the fans, respond the way you did for Ohio State, then I know this will be an amazing environment. Have a great weekend! Go Blue!

PENN STATE MEETING

The worst loss of the 2012-2013 basketball season belonged to us. Not something you enjoy typing, but our loss at Penn State was as bad as it gets. They didn't have a Big Ten win—we were fighting for our conference title lives—and it was ugly.

Give Penn State all the credit, they played terrific basketball, and we couldn't stop them. They ran same play over and over, and each time they got a different open look off it. When the buzzer rang, the locker room was the most devastated I had even seen. We all believed we'd blown our title chances, but more importantly, but for a team that was ranked Number 1 in the country weeks earlier, doubt had crept into our heads for the first time. Did this team peak too early? Could we get enough stops to win games?

I was one of the first guys to leave the locker room. It was depressing to be in a room with 25 very unhappy people. I was about to get on the bus and eat my chicken parmesan, but at the last minute I turned around and headed back in to the dressing room. As much as I wanted to be out of that depressing place, I needed to watch my teammates—especially the young guys—and make sure they knew this was not the end for us. We still had all our goals in front of us. But one after another, guys left for the bus and everyone had their earphones in and heads down. It was then I knew we had to have our first and only players-only meeting of the year. The air needed to be cleared, and this team needed to take a deep breath.

Everything had happened so fast. We started the year 16-0, and a week later ranked Number 1. While most teams hit adversity in November and December, we didn't hit it until February. Winning games in college basketball is incredibly hard and we made it look so easy for so long. We needed to refocus for this stretch run and some bad habits that had been formed needed to be cut out. I told Corey Person we needed to lay into some people; no more good cop. As close at this team was, we needed to stop worrying about not only being best friends, but also productive teammates.

So on that flight home from Happy Valley we booked a private room in the back of Pizza House. The leaders of the team: Tim, Trey, Corey and I, sat next to each other on the plane and made a list of things we wanted to be addressed. For one, a social media ban was being put into place. Twitter was gone, as we needed to limit distractions. We also needed to stop worrying about scoring points and just get stops. The biggest thing we decided was that the intensity was going to be turned up in practice, and if you didn't do your job, you were going to hear about it. Nothing was being pushed under the table anymore. This message came from Trey, who said he was taking it on himself to make sure practice was going to be a "you know what" if you didn't come ready. Corey went around the room and told everyone what they needed to do to help this team win, "EVERYONE has a key role, and you need to excel in that role."

After a 90-minute discussion on how this team was going to get to Atlanta, the final thing I said before we ate was this, "We don't have the time left in the season to have any more team meetings. You can see the light at the end of the tunnel, but it would be a real shame for a team that has all the parts to win a National Championship to blow it because they don't worry about the small things.

There are maybe eight teams who have a real shot to get to the Final Four. I mean, really good enough to get there, and we are one of them. We have the best backcourt in the country; the best freshman class in the country; the best team of centers, and a senior class that will lead us there. We can still live our dreams, but we've got to get back to Michigan Basketball!

After that everyone understood what needed to be done. We ate dinner and everyone went home knowing practice the next day was going to be like training camp; we would want it no other way. While a lot of things took place during the Final Four run, this meeting was the start of us getting back to Wolverine Excellence.

3/4/2013

THE GAME, THE FANS, FINISHING STRONG

What's up everyone?

I know, I know. It has been awhile. However, as you have seen, heard and read, we had this big stretch of the season when we were just so busy. Throw in school on top of that and, well, I just have not had the time to write.

But now I do!

What a day and what a game! Crisler Center was rocking and everyone that was there witnessed an epic battle between two great programs and teams. Even with our student section on spring break, our fans were energized and made a huge difference in the game. I can only imagine what next Sunday against Indiana will be like!

I'm not sure where to exactly start breaking down that game, but Trey (Burke) probably isn't a bad choice. I can break down all his stats, the five steals, but more than anything, it is about his will to win. Trey was not going to let us lose that game. He gets knocked down almost every possession going to the basket, but he gets right back up and sprints back on defense.

I really hope people don't take for granted just how great of shape he is in and how hard he competes because they marvel at the spectacular plays he makes. Do you know how exhausting it is to run off ball screen after ball screen and then play defense like he does? It is something else. There aren't many words to describe Trey, so I'll just say that I LOVE being his teammate!

The next guy I want to talk about is Glenn (Robinson III). Glenn has all the gifts in the world to be a special basketball player. He took a big step Sunday with his toughness. People throw that word around a lot, probably too much, but when you take a charge on Derrick Nix, that shows some toughness. We talked all week about taking charges and not backing out of the way. Sunday was a perfect example of that, because the game swung early in the second half due to those charges.

The other freshman who was terrific was Caris LeVert. Caris brings a defensive tenacity that changes the flow of the game. He gets into people and the Spartans went back on their heels a little bit. We need that nastiness and that edge every game from everyone on defense. It makes good teams great and great teams elite.

Sunday was a great win, but we play again Wednesday on the road against another hot team. Purdue just pulled off a great win at Wisconsin. Yes, at Wisconsin. We need to get back to playing Michigan basketball on the road. Purdue runs a ton of ball screens with guys who can really shoot, and our ball screen defense will be put to the test once again. It is our last road game of the season and we need to get a win in a hostile environment.

Finally, to all the fans that read the blog, I appreciate the emails. Good or sometimes bad, the passion you guys have for Michigan basketball is what makes playing for this school and program so special. The one thing you have to understand is winning games in college basketball, especially in the Big Ten, is incredibly difficult. Just look at all the upsets that take place every week. There is so much parity and the margin for error continues to get smaller.

At this time of the year, the key is having perspective and seeing the bigger picture. If you do that, you realize how exceptional this season has been and it's only going to get better. Hopefully I see many of you at senior night next weekend. Have a great week and Go Blue!

3/8/2013

SHORT AND SWEET

What's up everyone?

This blog is going to be short and sweet. As most of you know already, we pulled off a great road win on Wednesday night at Purdue. It was a total team effort. It sets up the biggest game of the year and lucky for us, it's at home.

All I could think about on the plane ride home was how electric our crowd is going to be!

This blog is an invitation to everyone who is going to be at the game on Sunday to arrive early and be loud! I don't care what you say, but as soon as Indiana takes the court, we need them to see thousands of people in Maize screaming at them.

My teammates and I are relying on all of you to make Sunday a really special day – something we will never forget, and I don't think you guys will either!

The journey to a Big Ten championship starts when we first get together in June. Everything seems so far off, but now with the game tipping off in 48 hours, there are no excuses. Fatigue, bumps and bruises – there is nothing that is going to stand in our way between us and a championship.

So to recap, wear maize, arrive early and be incredibly loud. I know we are going to lay it all on the line for you guys for a full 40 minutes. It is going to take a special effort to beat a great team like Indiana, but with your help, we can win championship No. 14!

Have a great weekend.

Go Blue!

MARCH MADNESS, BIG TEN WRAP-UP, NO SIRENS?

What's up everyone?

March Madness has arrived!

It doesn't matter if you are the No. 1 overall seed or the last team selected in – March Madness is all about the hope of making a special memory. I still get butterflies every time the brackets are announced. It might not be as nerve-racking as it was a couple years ago, but seeing Michigan flash across the board is something that never gets old.

For the last three years, every Saturday night before the bracket is announced, I watch the previous season's One Shining Moment. It gets you to realize how incredible the next month is going to be. From Cinderella stories to game-winning shots, this month is a young basketball player's dream growing up and now we are all living it!

That is the message for our team going forward. There is no pressure, a new season is starting and we are just going to have a ton of fun. We get to play in front of our home fans and hopefully Auburn Hills is full of fans rocking Maize and Blue. Thursday can't get here soon enough!

Reflecting on the Big Ten Tournament, I thought we played 70 really good minutes of basketball – the Penn State game and about 30 of the 40 minutes against Wisconsin. Unfortunately, when you play really good teams like the Badgers, you can't have bad stretches. Wisconsin is the definition of a solid team. They don't make mistakes to hurt themselves. You can beat them, but you have to play extremely hard and incredibly smart. This means the angles you take closing out, who you double off of and the rotations we are making.

We did those things at times really well in the game, which means we CAN do it. It would be one thing if we didn't see glimpses of playing sound solid defense in games, but we have done and will do it going forward! This is why I'm very confident we are going to make a run in the tournament. The light is going to go on for all of us and now it is just being consistent!

Off the court, the Big Ten Tournament and NCAA Tournament always make me wonder one big question. You always get a police escort to the games, but why don't the police turn its lights on?

What is the point of having an escort if you don't get to go through stop lights and make cars get out of the way? The police car just drives in front of us like any other car. It drives me crazy every time it happens and I always think maybe this year it will change. It never does!

With that it is off to class as I try to catch up on work with all the missed classes pilling up. I look forward to seeing a ton of you at the open practice on Wednesday and the game Thursday night.

We love playing at home, so let's make Auburn Hills Crisler Center West!

Have a great week!

Go Blue!

MEMORIES FOREVER, WE HAVE GUARDS, STANDING O'S

What's up everyone?

Dallas here we come!

What a weekend. I'm not sure where to exactly start, but the last two days are days I will never forget. I told the team about a month ago we can make memories that we can talk about for the rest of our lives, and while this magical ride is just starting, some memories have already been made!

I probably should start by talking about our fans. We had a huge home-court advantage. The Palace was rocking the entire game against VCU. There was more Maize and Blue in the stands than any other color, and we really appreciate that. Now we need all of you to come down to Dallas!

When we had our pregame talk before we took the court against VCU, Coach Beilein talked about all year long we have been preparing for this game. It started June 28 with the first drill we did this summer – a pivoting drill. It has continued all season long.

Coach Beilein is huge on working on your fundamentals so we don't turn the ball over. That means landing on two feet, catching the ball with two hands and always playing off your strong foot. He had a ton of confidence in our ability to handle the press because we train all season long for it.

Personally, I have a ton of confidence when the ball is in Trey's (Burke) hands or Spike's (Albrecht) or Tim's (Hardaway Jr.) or Nik's (Stauskas). We don't have good guards, we have great guards, and you guys all saw the show they put on handling the ball against VCU.

The VCU game and really for the past couple weeks was the Mitch (McGary) show. I'm so happy for him because he has worked so incredibly hard. I'm not just talking about getting extra reps in practice, but he has changed his diet, and it has made a huge impact in his game. It isn't easy to not have a dessert when the whole team is eating ice cream at a restaurant, but those sacrifices really pay off in the long run. Mitch has all the talent in the world, at his height not many people can do what he does, and you are just seeing now a whole year of hard work coming together.

I wish our fans could have all been in our locker room after the game. To see how much reaching the Sweet 16 means to our team and our program, you guys would all be very proud. We set a goal in our first team meeting to make it to the second weekend of the NCAA tournament.

The NCAA Tournament is a funny thing. You get selected, and it feels enormous. You have 68 teams in, so many sites, and really you are just worried about winning that first game. I will never forget my sophomore year when we lost to Duke how close and real it all feels once you can see yourself in the Sweet 16. While you always take it one game at a time, in one weekend you go from 64 teams to just 16 left. The journey we all dream about is right there, and now we just need to go get it!

The other part of the locker room that was pretty cool was giving every member of our staff a standing ovation because of all they do for us. People always ask me what's so special about playing at Michigan, and one of the responses I always give is the amount of people who go out of their way to make our student-athlete experience special. So after the game, guys like Pete Kahler (video analyst), who hadn't slept in days breaking down film, Kyle Barlow (graduate manager), C.J. Lee (administrative specialist), Travis Conlan (director of operations), Tom Wywrot (media relations), Bob Bland (equipment) and Tommy Jones (academics) all got an ovation from the team because of how much they mean to us. Obviously, our four coaches did an incredible job with the game plan, and I am convinced they never slept! Really, we would come down after sleeping, and they would be in the same spots, same positions working.

With that, I hope you guys are all excited for the week ahead. Enjoy the whole process leading up to the game because I know I am.

Have a great week and Go Blue!

THE SHOT

I think you all know what this entry is about. I knew it was going in as soon as Kansas missed that free throw and we had a chance. I bet my life on it and I'll explain why below, but first, I have watched those last 10 minutes multiple times and we played about as flawless as you could play. Kansas definitely helped us out at times, but what hit me the most was that we finally did everything we had talked about throughout the year about how to get back into games.. Instead of settling for tough threes, we got to the basket because teams don't want to foul at the end of games—you have to always attack. This was something emphasized after losing to Penn State because we settled for so many threes. We talked about finishing and taking our shot after the loss to Indiana; when Jordan Morgan dove on the floor and tossed it to Glenn for that ridiculous reverse layup, I thought back to Jordan's ball that didn't fall in at home vs. IU. We deserved that roll!

The point is this: when we talk to the media and say it will all come full circle, that the basketball gods will reward us and those losses will turn into learning experiences, well we aren't lying. I remember clearly, and I've gone back and watched the interview I had after that heartbreaking loss to Indiana at home. I said that in the long run, playing close games like this would pay off because there is an art to winning them. We painted the Mona Lisa against Kansas.

Now back to the shot. Everyone asks me now if I can predict the future, was I living two seconds ahead and knew the ball was going in? The answer is I wish I could predict the future, but instead I just knew who had the ball. Let's break down what Trey Burke did in two years: Freshman of the Year, Big Ten Champion, South Regional MVP, CONSENSUS player of the year; all he had left to do was hit an iconic shot. He had chances before; at Arkansas, at Ohio State, at Wisconsin, and at home vs. Indiana. There is no one else I would ever want taking a last second shot, so I knew he was due. Trey Burke had become an iconic figure at Michigan, now he just needed an iconic shot.

After all those misses mentioned above, I always told Trey, "You will make one when it matters most. When it's win or go home and all eyes are on you." I had been saying that since we lost to Arkansas his freshman year. So when he got the ball I told Blake and Matt, "I guarantee he makes this shot, I will bet my life on it." Now I didn't know he was going to pull up from around half court because I wouldn't bet my life on that, but as soon as he shot it, I jumped onto the court because that was the shot, the iconic shot he needed to seal his legacy.

As they say, the rest is history, but that game will be remembered for a long time as one of the greatest ever.

48 HOURS OF FUN, POWERADE BATH, HARLEM SHAKING

What's up everyone?

Atlanta here we come!

I have had to keep pinching myself to make sure I'm not dreaming because the last 48 hours has been about as magical as it can get. As a kid all 15 of us dreamed about cutting down nets and playing in the Final Four, and now that dream is going to become reality!

Everything really is bigger in Texas! From the police escorts with sirens, to Cowboys Stadium which is like a spaceship, to Trey's (Burke) shot from 30 feet to Nik (Stauskas) going 6-for-6, it was a massive weekend for Michigan basketball.

The Kansas game is the best basketball game I have ever been a part of. Simply put, it was one of the best games of all time. There was a time things really didn't look good, but the fat lady wasn't singing yet so we had time. I told the guys in the huddle let's do something magical, something people will talk about for years and years!

We just kept battling and battling, Glenn (Robinson III) with the Michael Jordan type steal and dunk, Jordan (Morgan) with the huge rebound on the floor, Tim (Hardaway Jr.) with the fast break dunk, and of course an iconic shot from an iconic player in an iconic game, Trey Burke is really good at basketball!

The second game is so much about coaching and getting as good of a game plan as you can get in 36 hours. Lucky for us, our coaching staff is as good as it gets when it comes to breaking down film and getting a plan in place. They don't sleep for about two days, but they find that fine line between getting stuff in, but not over doing it.

You have to just get enough in and with so many teams it comes down to knowing the team's personnel. The plays and actions are all great, but knowing which guys can shoot and which guys prefer to drive left or right it way more important.

You saw that plan in place against Florida. We switched all the screens on Eric Murphy so he didn't get off any open three's, we made their point guard finish around the basket instead of helping off shooters and we wanted to really get out and run in transition. The game plan was executed to perfection and when you can do that, very special things happen.

But what we did best all weekend was the celebration after the game! From each of us cutting get a piece of the net, to the shirts and hats to our families coming onto the court, to the Powerade bath we gave Coach B, it was all you dream about and more. Coach never saw the Powerade coming; he had no idea and at first was in shock and maybe a little upset. But Mrs. B gave us full permission and asked us to do it, so we have to listen to her!

The flight home was every bit as exciting. From rapping on the plane, to our Harlem Shake video which you all need to check it, we had a lot of fun! How many people can say they made a Harlem Shake video on the plane home from clinching a birth in the Final Four? Not bad timing!

Once we got off the plane, the celebration continued at the PDC with about a thousand fans waiting for us. With another police escort with sirens, we got off to everyone screaming. We thanked them all for coming and then headed home for the night!

With all the celebrating done, now it's time to get ready and move on to Syracuse. They are a great team who offers a ton of different challenges but we will be ready. At this point it sounds like everyone is going down to Atlanta, but we need more Maize and Blue than any other color in the Georgia Dome!

It is going to be a weekend you don't want to miss, something just like that Kansas game, you talk about for the rest of your life.

Have a great week and Go Blue!

Watch our Harlem Shake video at BlogIntoBook.com/harlemshake/
Watch our celebration video at BlogIntoBook.com/celebration/

FINAL FOUR WEEK

FINAL FOUR WEEK

The most surreal week of my life-and it probably won't ever change-was the week of the Final Four. As a kid growing up, you always dream of what it would be like to have police escorts, security guards, media days, and to play in front of seventy-five thousand people. I'm going to do my best to break down the week for you and all the things you would never know unless you were a part of it.

4/2/2013 MONDAY/TUESDAY:

The goal at the beginning of the week was to make it as normal as possible. We weren't going to leave for Atlanta until Wednesday. Monday was a total off day. Some guys had some treatment for bumps and bruises, but we didn't have any physical activity. However, the coaches wanted us to get all our tickets in by Tuesday. They knew how big of a distraction it would be and didn't want it hanging over our heads all week.

During this time, the coaches were meeting and beginning to set up a plan to beat Syracuse and their zone. They called coaching peers and began to understand the movements of the zone and what worked. They watched a ton of film, looked at what we did against zone defenses earlier in the year, and started deciding what areas of the zone we wanted to attack. I honestly believe that if you gave Coach B and the staff a week to prepare for a team it was going to be very hard to beat us. The plan they put in place was remarkable and I'll get more into it later.

Now one thing I conveyed was to soak in what the campus felt like. There was a buzz around campus that I couldn't even explain. You felt like a total rock star. From teachers asking to take pictures with you to kids stopping you in the street, all everyone talked about was when they were leaving for Atlanta and how they were getting there. Everyone in AA was wearing Maize and Blue. As players, we talked all the time about how one of the things we miss was what campus was like after a big game. The Diag being filled after Trey hit that three, the Brown Jug after the Florida game. We don't see how crazy it is, just hear about and see pictures. So the first two days of the week we wanted to make sure we understood how special this run was for the campus.

Tuesday was a normal day of practice. A little zone prep but mostly tons of skill work, as the coaches were still formulating a plan on how to attack Syracuse. We like doing our prep work for teams in two days; we weren't going to change that flow for the Final Four. The best part of Tuesday was the amount of gear we got. My God, I mean three new pairs of shoes, two new sweat suits, four new shirts, two shorts. Making the Final Four pays off in a lot of ways, but the gear was right up there!

We couldn't wait to leave for Atlanta. We came to practice all packed for the week Wednesday was aoother day of a ton of shooting, some defensive concepts on Syracuse, and then putting in the beginning of our plan on offense. We knew we wanted to get the ball to the middle, screen the top of the zone a ton, and make sure our shooters got to the corners. Those were the "themes" on how you beat the zone. Now we just needed the actions that would get us there.

For the NCAA tournament the NCAA provides the plane, so we weren't flying on our normal plane. The families of the coaches came with us, so it was a crowded plane, but players typically had a whole row to themselves. The flight only took about ninety minutes and we landed to a bus waiting for us on the tarmac as usual.

The team and coaches loaded into one bus and the families in the other. We then had a police escort to our hotel in Buckhead, located about twenty minutes from the Georgia Dome. Coach thought it was better to stay away from the craziness of Final Four week in downtown Atlanta—the right call. As we walked into the hotel through a private back entrance, a local college band was playing our fight song. Not a bad way to start the week. We all stayed on the same floor, with two or three on-duty policemen positioned 24/7 to make sure no one came to our floor who shouldn't be there. Our hotel layout was interesting in that it was an open hotel—you could see every room from the hallway. So when we would walk around, fans would take pictures of us and could see exactly what room we were staying in. We also traveled with two off-duty policemen who went everywhere with us. We felt very secure!

That night, like every night on the road, we had a snack before we headed to sleep: sandwiches and smoothies. We ate so well and so much on the road. Lights out and bed check was at 11:30 pm.

The first day of activities in Atlanta and it was jam-packed. We started with breakfast and a walkthrough, putting in actions to score against the zone. This would be the biggest test run preparing for Syracuse. Everything would be put in and we wanted to make sure it was sharp. We put in a ton of new sets and wrinkles we didn't run the whole year. The game plan looking back now was terrific. All in all I'd say we ran ten-to fifteen new actions, stuff we didn't really have in place before playing 'Cuse.

We then headed over to practice at the Georgia Dome. Coach B had managers and guys on scout team holding pads in the air to simulate the length of Syracuse. I thought it was a pretty sharp practice, considering how much new stuff was put in. The key was making sure Mitch had balance when he got the ball in the middle. He was such a terrific passer, we really thought he could pick the zone apart. I think you saw how that turned out.

After practice, we had media day. It was in a convention center connected to the Georgia Dome. They took us over in golf carts and most players had four-to five different responsibilities. The first part was all the stuff you see before the game. The promos with guys flexing and spinning the ball on their fingers. This all takes a ton of time and the cameras they use are crazy, with a ton of green screen. We took a ton of pictures and it was an exhausting process. This was also where you did the one-on-one interviews with Jim Nantz and Steve Kerr.

We then got golf-carted back to the locker room where hundreds of members of the media were waiting for us. This was always where you could get a few laughs with certain members of our team. Everyone wanted to break a story, some inside scoop, but mostly it was the same old clichés said over and over. Jon Horford did have the line of the Final Four though. It was in response to Brandon Triche, a player on Syracuse, saying earlier in the day he thought 'Cuse had mismatches at almost every position on the court. In response Jon said, "I would love to sit down and have a cup of tea with that young man and discuss the mismatches." There was nothing else to say!

After we finished with media, the official Final Four Kickoff began at Bracket Town. All the teams came together for an opening ceremony of sorts. This was the only time the whole week we spoke with members from other schools. We spent about an hour playing all the games that were in Bracket Town, from kicking soccer balls to making diving catches to hitting baseballs, we had a ton of fun. After that, we entered a theater where the opening ceremonies began. Jim Nantz was the MC and he introduced every team, showing clips of how each got to Atlanta. The coaches from each school went on stage and answered some questions, all in a very good mood to be there. Coach Beilein and Coach Boeheim go way back, and the story was told how Coach B got a coaching job from Boeheim calling on his behalf. We then got back on the buses, followed our police escort back to our hotel, and knew we were one day closer to playing.

4/5/2013 FRIDAY:

Friday was not nearly as hectic as Thursday. We had a bunch of meetings, going over our zone concepts, and also going over the Syracuse personnel. Syracuse didn't run a ton of complicated sets, they just had very talented players who tried to get buckets. The key was keeping them out of the paint and then rebounding. I was confident we could guard them, we just needed to make sure our offense didn't lead to fast-break points for them.

We then headed to the Georgia Dome for our open practice. This was when all the fans could watch us shoot around and run through some drills. It was very laid back and nothing important happened besides some guys trying to show off dunking. We did have the largest contingent of fans and they were loud, but that shouldn't surprise anyone. After our hour-long practice, we had our last media session before the game. At this point, there was nothing really new to say. The anticipation to play was incredibly high, but you couldn't get too geeked up when tip-off wasn't for thirty-six hours. It was a very long thirty-six hours.

Last but not least, we had a pep rally for our fans at the hotel. That was the first time you could sense the craziness from our fans. The ballroom of our hotel was packed; we had the band, cheerleaders, and fans from everywhere singing the fight song.

Coach B spoke and thanked everyone for coming, we shook some hands, and it was off to sleep. I doubt anyone slept much.

Final Four Saturday! We got to sleep in a little bit because we played the late game of the night. There was an incredible buzz in the hotel with Michigan fans everywhere decked out in Maize and Blue. We couldn't really walk down into the lobby without being swarmed, so the players stayed in a secure area, but it was hard not to check it out. Game day consisted of three or four different meetings: Offense, Defense, Special Situations, and then final thoughts. The plan was done, everyone knew how we were to beat Syracuse, now we just had to do it. We watched a ton of film, but it was really hard not to lose focus and start thinking about a night we had all dreamed of so many times. It didn't help getting hundreds of texts from family and friends, some giving advice on how to beat the zone and others on how hard they partied the night before.

We had about a forty minute shoot around at the Georgia Dome. Very, very light, almost just getting shots up, but we needed to leave the hotel and get some fresh air. Sitting around all day until 7 pm when our bus left would be torture. The mood was very relaxed, guys were joking around like it was the first day of practice.

The key was somehow finding a way to take a nap. You couldn't watch any TV stations because everyone was just breaking down the games and at this point I couldn't listen to it anymore. Around 6 pm, our uniforms got dropped off with the official Final Four sticker on them. There was no turning back now. The bus left around 6:30 pm, but the town was incredibly dead outside. Everyone was inside the stadium watching the first game or at a bar. The streets were empty as we took the twenty minute ride in.

I don't think I need to go into much detail as to what took place during that forty minute game. But in case you forgot. Mitch was Magic Johnson picking apart that zone, Caris and Spike hit huge threes, Jordan Morgan took an iconic charge, and Michigan fans took over downtown Atlanta for the night. Our game plan to let a 6'11" freshman who just began starting games a month ago break down the best zone in the country in the biggest game of his life worked.

Were you surprised? Honestly, I said it before, but you couldn't give our coaching staff a week to prepare for a team. It wasn't fair; they had this scheme down to a T.

We didn't get back to our hotel until around 2:30 am. Between another media session, guys getting cold tubs and figuring out some logistical issues, it was a long night, but we were all wide awake. The competition after the game was to see who had the most text messages on their phone. Don't quote me on this, but I think Mitch had around two hundred ten. I got a message from the Mayor of Chicago, so I was feeling good. The other thing that hit us was that we were playing for the National Championship, literally, in one day. You spend all season thinking about championship Monday and the Michigan Wolverines were there!

> Watch these "Great to be a Wolverine" chants in the arena:
> BlogIntoBook.com/michigan/great/
> BlogIntoBook.com/wolverine/

I think I fell asleep around 4:00 am. The fans were waiting for us back at the hotel, still packed in the lobby screaming our names and taking pictures. The coaching staff met and began preparations for Louisville. The breakdown for preparing for the second game of a tournament weekend goes as follows: Coach B won't spend one second looking ahead. So he didn't worry about VCU, Florida, or Louisville until after we won those first-round games. Each assistant was assigned a team we could play and it was their job to be ready to make a full presentation. Obviously, you couldn't prepare nearly as much as you would for a normal game, you just focused on the meat and potatoes. What they wanted to do on offense, the types of defenses they could play, and most importantly, learning about every player. Then present to the team in three sessions: offensive concepts, defensive concepts, and personnel. This was what took place all day Sunday.

We had a light practice back at the Georgia Dome as we made for our 100th trip there. It was mostly a walkthrough just trying to put in some of the plan for the following night. The pack of media waiting for us was nuts. From 68 to 64 to 32 to 16 to 8 to 4 to only 2 teams left they could write about. We were all trying to take in the moment, but it was so hard with the zoo that was going on around us.

Then for the first time all week, I got to see my family. All fifty of them—aunts, uncles, and cousins— came to our hotel. It was overwhelming, but something that I would never forget. For all of them to make the trip and be so excited to be part of this was truly surreal. I think I can speak for all my teammates when I say our families getting to live this dream with us made it way better.

We went out to dinner at a restaurant and I termed it the last supper. It kind of hit me there that this was the last time Team 96 would eat together. Most times teams don't really know when their season was going to end. You never expected to lose, which is why the season ending was always so hard. This was different: the last college basketball game of the year and we were playing in it. We ate at a steakhouse in a back private room, with all the patrons wondering why there were six cop cars located outside and people guarding the door.

As we got back to the hotel, I took some of the freshman aside and joked about how far we had come. From guys just trying to fit in during open gym, to now being crowned the Fresh Five, which I will never ever call them, it had been an amazing journey. I just needed to make sure they knew the moment was big, but no bigger than this team. The final message was this:

"When you run on that court, take a second, find your family and friends, smile because you are living a dream, and then go have the time of your life. 99.99% of kids growing up want to be in our shoes, let's go show them how fun it is."

Watch some more miscellaneous Final Four video footage at BlogIntoBook.com/michigan/misc/

The longest day of my life. It finally hit me what was going to take place in about twelve hours when I was watching ESPN. They were broadcasting live from Atlanta and were showing tweets from the likes of LeBron, Obama, and of course Kim Kardashian talking about the game. To think people of this stature would all be tuning in to watch us play gave me the chills. The truth was, legends were going to be made tonight.

The day was going to be just like Saturday. Watch film in different segments, go for a shoot around, take a nap, and somehow waste enough time for the game to start at 9:30 pm.

Everyone wanted to talk about Louisville's defense vs. our offense. No doubt that was a key, but our offense was so potent because we could score quickly. In order to score quickly you have to get stops and rebounds. The key for me was getting easy baskets against them by getting stops. It was too exhausting to go against their pressure D all game.

Last time we drove to the Dome Atlanta it was empty—on this night it was a scene from a movie. As our motorcade made our final trip to the Dome, the streets were packed with fans walking to the game. News trucks parked for miles and people broadcasting live from outside. Everyone waving at our bus, just trying to take in the scene.

I refuse to go much into the game, as I have never watched it in its entirety. I know this: we were up 39-27 and playing great. Luke Hancock hit four straight threes, of which I believe two were bad coverage. Spike became a legend and if we would have won that game, I'm not sure whom he would be dating, but I would have made him retire because you can't top that.

The second half I believe we had some tough luck. Dieng hit some shots that literally died on the rim and we missed some easy opportunities we would convert most of the time.

Watch some pre-game videos from the fans:
BlogIntoBook.com/michigan/cheer/
BlogIntoBook.com/pregame/

Q: UM Hoops: *The Fab Five were all there, and four of them came into the locker room after the National Championship. What did you make of them joining you guys in the locker room?*

A: J-Bart: At first, it was a little like, what are these guys doing here, they haven't been a part of this team or a part of this program for a really long time. But then, once all the media cleared out they spoke.

I thought Juwan (Howard) really had a great message: they were here for us. They were here to link Michigan past and the present and the future together. And he said one of the greatest accomplishments this team will have is bringing Michigan basketball back.

They weren't there to talk to the media, they weren't there for themselves. They were there to support us and Michigan basketball. They came around and gave everyone a hug, and they said that if any of us ever need anything from them they'll be here, whether it's advice about basketball or life, they're here for us.

I think after initially feeling like they were here for the media circus of it, they were here because they loved what we stood for and loved how we played. I think that meant a lot to us. Juwan did a great job with it.

Thanks to UMHoops.com for contributing this Q&A

THE FINAL ENTRY

What's up everyone?

I will never forget the day I first talked to John Beilein. I was walking to the cafeteria at Phillips Exeter, and I knew I needed to make a good pitch to get Coach B to want me at Michigan. We started talking and he asked me "Why Michigan? Why turn down scholarship offers? Why turn down guaranteed playing time to come to a place where nothing was guaranteed?"

He thought he got me, but I responded, "Coach, I want to be a part of something bigger than myself." There was no response, just silence on the phone. I knew I got Coach B and from there a dream, a fairytale for four years, started!

I grew up in Highland Park, Ill., right in the middle of Big Ten country. The dream was always to play in the best conference in the world. To play in front of 15,000 screaming fans who either love you or hate you, to fly in charter plans and stay at five-star hotels.

The thousands and thousands of shots I took with my dad, from summer days in the 90s to those cold fall nights when I just wanted to be a "normal" kid in the driveway, always had me playing somewhere in the Big Ten. When he counted down three, two and one and I took the last shot, I pictured myself on this stage. There were some, probably even many, times I hated being on that driveway, when my dad would keep saying "one more" but trying to live out dreams takes hard work.

Now when I said I wanted to be a part of something bigger than myself, sure it was true, but it was also a great answer to give a coach. At the same time, I had no idea how big Michigan was, how much bigger than me this brand is.

Because of basketball, I've been to Amsterdam, Belgium, Paris, Maui, New York, Orlando, Dallas, Nashville, Charlotte, New York and Brooklyn just to name a few cities. The hundreds of people who work here just to make sure your student-athlete experience is as good as it can possibly be. I've met more fans and alumni who are just so proud to be associated with the Block 'M' and Michigan that all they want to do is just shake your hand.

The last four weeks I've received more emails, more texts and been stopped on the street just so people could tell me they loved our team because they represented everything that is right with Michigan. I knew people would love this team long before and for so many different reasons.

I knew the 96th team at Michigan could be special, very special.

It took me about two weeks into the summer to see we had all the pieces, the best backcourt in the country, an incredible freshman class that were GREAT guys, and I knew the leadership would not be a problem because of our senior class. There is one thing that separates good college teams from great ones when you have elite-level talent. It's chemistry. It is the most cliché thing in the world, but I mean it in a totally different way. I don't mean guys high-fiving each other and respecting one another.

That doesn't do anything. I'm talking about guys really understanding who each one of us are. What has Josh Bartelstein been through that shapes him as a person for good and bad?

What makes high school basketball so fun is that you get to play with your best friends. Guys you grew up with for 18 years and dreamed about playing with. In college, each team is together for one year. You don't really know each other as anything else besides an athlete. Before we played a game this year, in mid-September, we did an exercise with Greg Harden.

This prompt was simple: What is the best and toughest experience that has happened to you in the last two years and it could have nothing to do with basketball? For some teams, they wouldn't take this seriously, but we were in our locker room for hours. There were tears of joy and tears of agony, guys opening up about things you would never wish on your worst enemy – moments where guys couldn't get the words out, where all you wanted to do was hug your teammate.

The next day I walked into Coach Jordan's office and said when we look back on this season in six months, yesterday will be a moment that shaped this team. We began to see each other as people, not just athletes who were brought together, but true friends who were developing a love for one another because we understood who we all were.

I can't tell you how many times I've pinched myself in the last three weeks to make sure my dream was real. When I climbed the ladder to cut down the nets in the Elite Eight, when my family was on stage with me in Dallas, when I woke up the next morning in Ann Arbor, when we landed in Atlanta, okay I think you get the point.

This was always the plan. I told our team after we lost at Wisconsin, on that half-court shot; WE WERE going to make memories that lasted a lifetime. We had six weeks left in our season, and you could for the first time see the light at the end of the tunnel. If everyone bought in and just did all the small things that make great teams elite, we could end our journey in Atlanta. There would be more bumps in the road for sure, but a vision on where our journey was going to end; a final destination was established on that day.

We made it to the final game, the last stop. It was magical, a fairytale that for some reason didn't have a happy ending. But so many times in team sports the journey is forgotten too much of the time. I took so many pictures and so many videos on my phone because I never wanted this week to end. It wasn't the games I was most worried about missing, but the interaction at team dinners, Corey (Person) making fun of Eso (Akunne) and Eso making fun of Corey, Mitch (McGary) dancing and (Jon) Horford just being Horford.

Many times basketball is over-complicated. There are so many "experts" out there who try and tell you all the secret things that will win a game. It really is a simple game. Louisville is a great team and in the second half we couldn't get stops. There guards are incredibly quick, there big men are incredibly strong, and Luke Hancock doesn't miss. We had control of that game but when someone hits four straight threes the game changes. That's it.

When the final buzzer went off, the confetti was released and the fireworks went off, I took one last look at what 75,000 people looked like – half of them in total jubilation and half in total devastation. I looked at my family all 50 of them who made the trip, and I smiled because they got to be a part of my dream.

Once we got into our locker room, it was just as sad as that team bonding experience with Greg Harden. When your leader, Coach B, gets chocked up, you know it's going to be really tough. Some guys spoke, and the message was pretty much always the same.

The love we had for each other, the memories we made would never be forgotten. I told my guys for the rest of my life if they EVER needed anything I would ALWAYS be there. We were brothers now. I care about every one of them like I do my three sisters, and we shared something that one day when the time is right we will all consider ourselves champions. We then sang the greatest fight song in the world one last time, and it was one of the hardest things I've ever had to do.

I knew I had about five minutes before the media came in, and I sat in my chair with tears running down my face and a towel over my head. I pinched myself one last time this time hoping I was dreaming, but the moment was real. My story was coming to an end, 23 years worth of basketball, 23 years of my life being dedicated to a sport I loved. Then I remembered this is so much bigger than me, bigger than my whole family contingent, bigger than us 15, bigger than our program.

This is for the University of Michigan.

I get the chills as I write this, but we made it so our fans can hold their heads up high when they speak of Michigan basketball. We brought the Fab Five back into the same stadium again. We gave you guys one great run and had the time of our lives doing so!

That's it for me. My last blog.

I need to thank Tom Wywrot for all the help and letting me do this, no doubt the best SID in the business. It has been three great years; I can't thank you all enough for reading. I'm keeping each and every blog entry as a book because the ride has been surreal. This program is back, and it's never going away.

But now I need one favor from you.

Forever and Always
Josh
Go Blue!

2012-13 Michigan Basketball Roster

No.	Wolverine	Pos.	Hgt.	Wgt.	Hometown (High School)
1	Glenn Robinson III	F	6-6	210	St.John, Ind. (Lake Central)
2	Michael "Spike" Albrecht	G	5-11	170	Crown Point, Ind. (Northfield Mount Hermon Prep [Mass.])
3	Trey Burke	G	6-0	190	Columbus ,Ohio (Northland)
4	Mitch McGary	F	6-10	250	Chesterton, Ind.(Brewster Academy [N.H.])
5	Eso Akunne	G	6-2	225	Ann Arbor, Mich. (Father Gabriel Richard)
10	Tim Hardaway Jr.	G	6-6	205	Miami, Fla. (Palmetto Senior)
11	Nik Stauskas	G	6-6	190	Mississauga, Ontario, Canada (St. Mark's School[Mass.])
13	Matt Vogrich	G	6-4	200	Lake Forest, Ill. (Lake Forest)
15	Jon Horford	F	6-10	250	Grand Ledge, Mich. (Grand Ledge)
20	Josh Bartelstein	G	6-3	210	Highland Park, Ill. (Phillips Exeter Academy [N.H.])
22	Blake McLimans	F	6-10	240	Hamburg, N.Y. (Worcester Academy [Mass.])
23	Caris LeVert	G	6-5	170	Pickerington, Ohio (Central)
32	Corey Person	G	6-3	210	Kalamazoo, Mich. (Central)
44	Max Bielfeldt	F	6-7	245	Peoria, Ill. (Notre Dame)
52	Jordan Morgan	F	6-8	250	Detroit, Mich. (University of Detroit Jesuit)

Michigan Basketball Staff

Head Coach John Beilein (6th season)
Assistant Coach Jeff Meyer
Assistant Coach Bacari Alexander
Assistant Coach LaVall Jordan
Director of Basketball Operations Travis Conlan
Administrative Specialist C.J. Lee
Strength & Conditioning Coach Jon Sanderson
Athletic Trainer John DoRosario
Video Analyst Peter Kahler
Graduate Manager Kyle Barlow

Class Breakdown

Fifth-Year Senior (1):	Corey Person
Senior (4):	Eso Akunne, Josh Bartelstein, Blake McLimans, Matt Vogrich
Redshirt-Junior (1):	Jordan Morgan
Junior (1):	Tim Hardaway Jr.
Redshirt-Sophomore (1):	Jon Horford
Sophomore (1):	Trey Burke
Redshirt-Freshman (1):	Max Bielfeldt
Freshman (5):	Spike Albrecht, Caris LeVert, Mitch McGary, Glenn Robinson III, Nik Stauskas

ABOUT THE AUTHOR

Josh Bartelstein was the creator and author of the "Bartelstein Blog" featured on the Mgoblue website for the past 3 years. After fielding many requests, he has connected many of the blogs from the memorable championship season, along with video, highlight pictures and additions from teammates, into a book. Bartelstein was the captain of the 2012-2013 University of Michigan basketball team that made an appearance in the NCAA national championship after a 25-year drought. In addition to the Final Four appearance, Bartelstein was also a part of the University of Michigan basketball team that captured the Big 10 title in 2012. Bartelstein was born in Chicago and grew up in Highland Park, IL. He is the oldest of four children including three younger sisters; Morgan, Courtney and Kirby. Josh is 25 years old and moved back to Highland Park after graduating with a Sports Management degree from the University of Michigan. Bartelstein chose to document the road to success of the Michigan basketball team to offer the many passionate Wolverine fans an inside look into the team, both on and off the court.

Made in the USA
Lexington, KY
20 January 2015